PELICAN BOOK

A735

YOUR GROWING CHILD AND RELIGION

R. S. LEE

Roy Stuart Lee was born in Stuart Town in New South Wales. He was educated at Orange High School, Sydney University, and Oxford University, and received an M.A., a B.Litt., and a D.Phil. He was the Vice-Warden of St John's College, Morpeth, in New South Wales and then came to London, where he was the Overseas Religious Broadcasting Organizer for the B.B.C. From 1947–61, he was the vicar of the University Church of St Mary the Virgin, Oxford, and the chaplain of Nuffield College, Oxford. He is now a fellow and chaplain of St Catherine's College, Oxford, and continues also as chaplain of Nuffield College.

Roy Lee has also published *Freud and Christianity* and *Religion and Worship*, and has contributed to various periodicals. He is married and has two daughters.

R. S. LEE

YOUR GROWING CHILD AND RELIGION

A Psychological Account

PENGUIN BOOKS

Penguin Books Ltd, Harmondsworth, Middlesex, England
Penguin Books Pty Ltd, Ringwood, Victoria, Australia

—

First published in the U.S.A. by Macmillan 1963
Published in Pelican Books 1965

—

—

Made and printed in Great Britain
by Hazell Watson & Viney Ltd
Aylesbury, Bucks
Set in Linotype Baskerville

CONTENTS

PREFACE

THIS book has been written in the hope that it may be of some use to all who are involved in the religious education of children, that is, parents, teachers, clergy, Sunday-school teachers, and so on. It may be of interest to a wider public because it has to deal with the fundamental phases of the growth of personality in children, since religion cannot be separated from the general development of the child.

It is not a handbook to provide rules and syllabuses by which religious education may be carried out. The aim of the book is to show that these are secondary to a much more fundamental matter, namely, what is in the mind of the child to enable him to absorb any teaching given. It is of first importance to understand how the child thinks and feels at each stage of his growth so that we can shape religious teaching to fit his emotional needs and his capacity to interpret correctly what is said to him. It is on this that the book lays emphasis. Because it is not written for specialists in psychology but for the help of those who are responsible directly for bringing children up in religion, it has simplified, perhaps oversimplified, what is an exceedingly complex study. For the same reason, frequent recapitulations are included in the various chapters, at the risk of boring those who are familiar with psychological concepts.

It is to be noted that theology is not discussed in the book. Its approach is purely psychological, and the place and value of religion are taken for granted. Psychology is not a substitute for religion; but on the other hand religious behaviour obeys psychological laws, and it is disastrous to ignore these. It is to them that attention is drawn. Because readers who may be interested in the general question of how theology and psychology are related will find many excellent books on the subject, the point is not raised in these pages.

I wish to acknowledge my gratitude to Dr D. W. Winnicott and the Tavistock Publications and to Dr G. F. Morton and Duckworth & Co. for permission to use the quotations in Chapter 11.

Oxford R. S. LEE

PART 1

The Foundations

CHAPTER 1

THE MEANING OF RELIGIOUS DEVELOPMENT

A FEW years ago a new wing was added to Nuffield College, Oxford, to complete the quadrangle. It was of special interest to me because it was to contain the chapel. For over a year I watched the work from my window opposite. The builders spent a great deal of time and effort in laying the foundations. For long months workmen were excavating, driving in piles, pouring in concrete, laying bricks; and it seemed that the college would never get built. At last the foundations came up to the level of the ground floor, but even then they did not look like a building. However, in due course the new wing was finished, and we have a fine quadrangle. It looks now as we expect a college to look, and we can be proud of it and confident that it will stand for centuries, like the other colleges of Oxford.

This has been a parable to me about the subject of this book, in which I want to share with my readers, particularly parents of young children and others who have the responsibility of training them, some of my reflections about the religious development of children.

Let us get clear from the start what we mean by religious development. It may possibly be taken to mean only the end product, the religious life that is attained after and as the result of growing through childhood to adulthood. That is too narrow a meaning. I use it to describe all that is involved in the process of growth of the mind by which we acquire a religious attitude to life, and I propose to discuss how men and women come to hold the beliefs, sentiments, and practices we call religious. I shall not attempt to define what we mean by religion, for this book is not an essay in philosophy but a description of practical matter of fact, and we all recognize what 'religious' means. There are borderline cases where we may be doubtful whether or not we are dealing with religion, but we shall not be concerned with those. We may assume that a newborn baby has no religion. What are the steps by which he develops it?

To some people that question seems the same as asking what the proper form of religious instruction is. They have in mind the vision of parents kneeling or standing by the baby's cot, saying their prayers so that the child will be familiar with prayer from the beginning of his life; or they want to know how soon and in what way the child can be taught to pray; when he should be taken to church or Sunday school; how much Bible instruction should be given to him: how God should be explained to him; and other such matters. They assume without query that these are the important things; that when you talk about the religious development of the child you are primarily concerned with the techniques of teaching him the beliefs and practices of religion. When parents ask me to tell them how to teach their young children religion, and I reply that the best thing they can do to this end is to give them as little religious instruction as possible until they are over seven years of age, I am usually met with an incredulous stare, or the parents think I am joking. Of course, the technique of religious instruction is important, but there is something more important in the religious development of the child. It lies in what the child becomes rather than in what he is told. Religion is much more a matter of what a man or woman is than what he believes or does. It is an attitude of mind and heart and will lie in the shape of the self, the personality, rather than in a set of doctrines and rules of conduct that are believed or followed. These latter can be taught; the other can only be fostered.

The problem to which we should address ourselves is how to promote this growth from within. Unless that is effected, religious instruction will impose only a superficial layer upon the personality of the child, and his religion will be a veneer, without any depth. That is the problem to which I want to suggest the answers in this book. So I say at the beginning that religious development begins from birth, or even before birth, but religious instruction, in the technical sense of teaching about religion, should not begin for many years.

Religious development is like the building of a college. There is a long period when the foundations are being laid, when what is going on does not look at all like the finished product. Just as the laying of the foundations of a building may seem to occupy a disproportionate time, so in the growing child a considerable period has to be passed before there is anything that can properly be called religious. William James, the greatest of American psychologists, quite rightly said that the healthy young child is a pagan.

If the builders had tried to erect the college on inadequate and badly prepared foundations, or before the foundations were ready to take the building, it would soon collapse. So, too, a religious life reared upon inadequate or unsettled foundations will be in danger of breaking down. Hence the first part of a child's life must be devoted to laying the foundations for the religious life that will come later, and only when the foundations are properly laid can the work of building up the religious life proper be safely attempted.

The first seven years constitute the period for laying the foundations of religion. This is the most important period in the whole of a person's life in determining his later religious attitudes. On the foundations being laid then, the whole superstructure of his religious life will be built. In a building, the shape of the foundations determines or limits the shape of the superstructure and the weight they can carry. So it is with the personality. The general pattern of the personality is being shaped in this early period, and the pattern will endure. To say this does not take away the importance of later developments. A house erected on the foundations laid may be of wood, brick, stone, concrete, or other material, and it may be used as a dwelling place, a shop, a community centre, or any one of many other purposes. Similarly, the groundwork pattern of personality that is laid in infancy is capable of leading to many different kinds of character, according to the circumstances entering into that person's history; different, that is to say, socially, economically, professionally, culturally, but all having the same basic psychological pattern.

The possibility of variation on the same foundation should not be allowed to blind us to the necessity of having a foundation. The greater the building that has to be erected, the greater the need that the foundation be good. Religion is the most inclusive and most far-reaching aspect of life, and requires adequate foundations. Just as the foundations of a building are unlike the superstructure, so the foundations of religion are not themselves religious. Their function is to make religion possible in the subsequent years.

In this early period the child passes through a number of stages in which he is totally preoccupied in discovering himself, his family, and the world about him. By fulfilling this task he acquires the means necessary to go on to the further discovery, that of God. If he attempts, or is pressed to attempt, the exploration of God before he is ready for it, the result can be serious, preventing him from ever making the attempt successfully. It is difficult enough to grow healthily through the normal stages of infancy, without having this extra and impossible task thrust upon him. If he does negotiate the first seven years with reasonable success, he is ready to begin the next task.

Already it is clear that my metaphor is breaking down. A building does not grow; it has to be made by the work done on it. A child, and a child's mind, grow spontaneously. It is true that this growth is stimulated by the impact of other people and the world in general upon him, but these do not cause the growth; they only influence it, help to turn it in this or that direction. The growth comes from within the child. Nevertheless, the metaphor of building is valuable to draw attention to the need to have a period of mental development before we try to turn the growth openly into religious forms.

The first step, therefore, in tracing out the religious development of the child is to find out how his mind takes shape in this early period, that is, how he thinks, feels, desires; what the mental equipment is that he has built up, and how he uses it in his progressive mastery of the world. The first half of this book will be devoted mainly to that. It will be concerned with the stages of growth of the child's mind and personality. In this half we shall be concerned with foundations, and little will be said directly about religion. There will be brief indications about the way in which what is going on in the child's mind has potentialities for his later religious life, but the exposition of them will be deferred to the second half.

This procedure is necessary for the sake of clarity of exposition, but it raises one difficult matter. Many of the references will be to the dangers that arise from wrong teaching or treatment of children, dangers, that is, of creating a false or arrested religion, a pseudo-religion that may be mistaken for true religion. This opens up an enormous field, far too wide to be attempted in this book. Apart, therefore, from occasional indications of how development may go wrong, this part of the book will be confined to what it is usual to call the normal, or healthy, development, that is, that which leads on to a fully mature and integrated personality. We know that many aberrations and fixations take place that prevent this full development, but they must be put aside. It is difficult enough to follow the complexity of the main line of growth, and it is that which it is most important to understand. It is to be hoped, however, that insight into what is happening in the mind of the normal child will give some understanding of the abnormal.

In the second half of the book more practical advice will be given, both on how to treat small children and on the best methods of religious instruction. First we must understand what is happening within the child. He is a living, growing personality, and unless we take full account of that, our training is sure to go astray, whether it be for religion or anything else. His religion must grow up within him as an integral part of him. It must be his own, not something lived by him second-hand.

CHAPTER 2

WHAT IS A BABY?

IN setting out to explore the religious development of children, it seems logical to start from the beginning of a child's life. At once we come up against the difficulty of saying when that is. Is it the moment of birth when the child's body is separated from that of his mother? (We shall use the word 'him' and 'his' instead of the impersonal 'it' and 'its', to include both boy and girl, unless it becomes important to distinguish the sex, in which case the meaning will be made clear). Obviously, in one sense a child's life begins with his birth. Before that, however, he has been living in his mother's womb for nine months as part of her, yet a very special part, with something like independence. Shall we then count the moment of conception as the beginning of the child's life? Even this is arbitrary, for the ovum from which he developed after its fertilization by the male sperm was in existence as an integral part of his mother, contributing its quota to her physical and mental life. If we trace back the origins of the ovum, we are led to the beginning of the mother, and the same questions arise with regard to her. There is no absolute point at which we can say, 'Here the child began to live.' We can say only that he is part of the stream of life that focuses in each individual and is handed on from individual to individual.

This is not an abstract academic point I am raising. On the contrary, it is one of great practical importance, and neglect of it is the cause of much false thinking about the nature of human life. It draws attention to three principles that govern the development of a human being and form a framework or perspective in which we must always set the individuality of any person when we are seeking to understand what he is and how he came to be what he is. To try to understand an individual simply as an isolated unit is to be certain of misunderstanding him.

The three principles to which I refer are the principles of growth, of inheritance, and of relationship. What they mean will be shown more fully as we proceed, but it is worth while to pause here and look briefly at them.

To be alive means to grow in body and in mind. The seed grows into a plant, the egg into a chicken, the human ovum into a baby and by stages into the full-grown man. When the body reaches maturity of development and major enlargements cease, it still goes on replacing dead cells with fresh living ones. The mind adds the experiences of today to those of yesterday and the days before yesterday. Death puts an end to this process of growth so far as life in this sphere of existence is concerned. The body decays; the mind disappears. There is change still going on in the dead body, but that is not what we mean by the growth of that individual organism.

There are two aspects of growth that are important to note here. The first is that growth always requires the taking into the self of some part of the external world. The body takes in food and drink, air, light and heat radiations, and other subtle parts of the external world. It incorporates these and transmutes them to make them part of itself, using them to form the cells of the body or to supply the various forms of energy the body requires. Similarly, the mind grows by taking into itself the various experiences it is capable of receiving from within its body (and the body is external in some sense to the mind) and through the organs of the body from the outside world. Without this mental food the mind cannot grow. Growth, therefore, both of body and mind, depends on the individual organism reaching out, consciously or unconsciously, towards the world, to take it or part of it into itself.

The second aspect of growth to which I referred is related to this. There is an inner urge or compulsion to grow. This is, as we say, a law of nature. Deprivation, disease, or accident may hinder or distort parts of the growth, but only death stops it. Life is always dynamic, striving towards something. Some have tried to explain this as a 'life force' or *élan vital,* or 'life instinct', but this is not to explain it; it is only to give a name to this character of life, namely, that it entails growth. We may leave the explanation to theologians and philosophers, and simply note the fact that the baby grows and cannot be stopped from growing except by death. We note, too, that the growth is according to a general pattern that is likewise inherent in all living organisms. A kitten cannot become a dog, nor a puppy a cat. Each organism fulfils the law of its kind. The moth is first an egg, then a caterpillar, then a pupa, before it becomes a moth. It does not select the stages of its growth. It inevitably follows the pattern of its kind. So the human baby grows through the stages that are peculiar to mankind, each stage preparing the way for the next.

The energy for this growth comes in the first place from the food the baby takes and converts by its bodily processes to its own use. This energy is channelled into action through a bundle of instinctive dispositions. The baby does not act at random, but is supplied at birth with the psychological mechanisms that dispose him to carry out those actions that are necessary to his continued existence. These are instinctive; that is, not learned from experience, though they may be improved by experience.

The word 'mechanisms' is used to describe these dispositions for want of a better term, but we must be careful not to think of this as machinery. Machinery does not grow, whereas these dispositions do grow, in man, at any rate. In the lower animals the dispositions seem to be relatively fixed, particularly in the insect world, so that the creature does not have to learn how to carry out quite complicated chains of behaviour. The dispositions with which a human baby is provided are not nearly so definite. They prompt to necessary lines of behaviour, such as taking food, but the baby has to learn most of the detailed forms of action. Hence, the baby is endowed with a different type of mind, one capable of assimilating experience and learning from it how to vary and improve behaviour, and therefore his behaviour is not so fixed and definite as it is in lower animals. Nevertheless, the broad channels are there to direct the energy generated towards appropriate kinds of action.

We shall have to consider the different instincts, and how they develop, in the pages that follow. Here it is important to note that a baby is not a passive object, weak and helpless as he may seem, but is a living dynamo, generating energy at an increasing rate that will drive him to action upon the world. The way he will act will be the result of the native dispositions with which he is endowed at birth becoming modified and redirected as a result of his capacity to learn from experience. This is a highly complex development.

Human beings grow according to the general pattern of human beings. In a sense we may say that they inherit this law of growth that controls them. But there is another, narrower sense in which inheritance is important, and this brings us to the second of our three main principles.

A baby does not start his life from nothing, but inherits from his parents the complex set of tendencies referred to just now, that will shape and control the directions in which he grows. They require the stimulus of the environment, which is equally necessary to growth, as we have already seen, and about which much more will have to be said at a later point; but the inherited factors set limits to what nurture can do with the child, prompting growth in one direction, barring it in another. The physiological means through which these inherited factors are conveyed are the genes derived from the parents. The number of genes is so large in the human being, and the possibility of variation so infinite, that no two individuals are ever the same. Hence, while all men share the general pattern of humanity, within that general pattern each person has his own individual pattern, determined by his heredity and conditioned by the detailed circumstances of his life.

For the third principle I have used the term 'relationship'. It refers to the fact that an individual is acted upon by his environment, the world other than himself, and in turn acts upon it or reacts to its action. To speak of a man's environment can be unintentionally misleading, for it emphasizes the spatial relationship too much and makes man and his environment too external to each other. The environment is depicted as surrounding the individual. This falsifies the reality. Contact with the world is always by some mode of incorporation. We have already noted that to go on living a man has to swallow food and drink, part of his environment. Similarly, his mind takes into itself that which he comes to know, by way of sensations, perceptions, ideas. And just as we take the world into ourselves by knowing it, so also we enter into the world by the act of knowing it. It is a mutual relationship. Similarly, in our emotional relationships, such as love, for instance, we live in and desire to be lived in by the object of our love. Every aspect of living is a relationship of some kind by which the world is in us and we are in the world.

The importance of this principle will be made clearer as we proceed. In the young child it can be seen more easily than in an adult, because the child lives in a limited world, comprising mostly his family and his home, and the impact of that world upon him is relatively simple to observe. We can watch the growth of his self or his personality and see how it follows the lines of expanding relationships with the world, as step by step he gets to know more of it; we can see how these relationships both stimulate and feed his inborn capacities until what was potentially in him becomes actuality. In growing, the child takes the world into himself and makes it his own, but the corollary inevitably holds that he thereby becomes another individuation of the world. It has entered into him to make him what he is.

If we believe that God is the ultimate meaning of the world, then we must also believe that the fullness of human development is reached only when a man is filled with God, possesses him, and is possessed by him. In this mutual possession the individual becomes a special manifestation of God, in which there is mutual indwelling. This is the climax of growth in religion.

The way to it is a long and complicated growth in which the mind and the heart and the will are gradually developed and stretched until they are capable of seeing God as he is, knowing him, loving him, and serving him. It is the stages of this growth that we shall attempt to trace.

CHAPTER 3

PRE-NATAL INFLUENCES

A CHILD'S existence as an individual begins at the moment of conception, when the father's sperm unites with the mother's ovum. Because these are living cells, at conception he, as it were, takes over the contributions of life from his parents and begins to be a new unit of life. He takes from each of them as an inheritance, but deprives them of nothing. Instead, they come to life again in him.

This is only the beginning of independence. His father will make no more direct contributions to him until after he is born, but he continues to be physically dependent on his mother's body during the period of gestation in the womb and for some time after his birth. He draws from her body the nourishment by which he grows. Her body protects and warms and feeds him.

Nothing is known about what mental contribution is made to the embryo by the state of the mother's mind during pregnancy. We can only hazard uncertain guesses about what will be the effect on the unborn child if, for instance, the mother undergoes some experience that terrifies her, or if she is subjected to prolonged anxieties. There is a quite widespread belief that the mother's thoughts and feelings can influence him, but there is not nearly enough evidence to prove that there is any direct mental communication from mother to child. The belief need not be dismissed as an old wives' fable, but it must be treated as a very uncertain speculation.

On the other hand, we know that changing mental states, especially where strong emotions are involved, bring about or are accompanied by corresponding changes in the body, by glandular secretions, altered blood pressure, muscular tensions, nervous discharges, and so on. We can readily suppose that such changes in the mother's body will to some extent also affect the embryo growing in her womb, in spite of the insulation the womb provides. We know that if the mother has German measles during the first six weeks of pregnancy, it may affect the baby's sight or hearing. And the use of the drug thalidomide as a tranquillizer by pregnant women has been followed by a large number of deformed children. If, however, the mother has a relaxed, tranquil, and happy state of mind, she will probably be then providing the best physiological environment for the bodily welfare of the embryo, and, at the same time, any possible mental influence she may have on him will be most favourable, whether it comes directly through some form of mental transmission or indirectly through changes in the functioning of her body that are felt by the unborn child. There is no proof of these suppositions, but they are reasonable ones, and therefore probably correct.

If they are well founded – and we would be wise to take them into account – the period of pregnancy is not merely a time in which the child by his growth is getting ready to leave the mother's body; in it, external influences have already begun to shape his future character. And the fact of being pregnant has an enormous effect on the mother's mental outlook (which includes feelings and desires as well as thoughts). Both consciously and unconsciously she prepares to give birth to her baby, and the attitudes she adopts will largely determine what kind of treatment the child will receive after he is born, as well as having an influence on him in the womb.

When a woman knows that she is pregnant, her emotions are very complex, and it is safe to say that no two women react in precisely the same way. A great deal depends upon the character of the particular woman and the circumstances of her life. Her body has been prepared by nature to bear a child; so, too, has her mental outlook been formed to dispose her to care for the child. This biological instinct leads her to centre her thoughts and feelings around the baby that is taking shape in her body. He becomes a factor that must be taken into account in everything she does.

Inevitably some of her interest and attention is withdrawn from other things and she may even seem to grow self-centred. She tends to become more dependent on her husband, needing to be protected and guided by him, both physically and mentally. If she does not get the care and solicitude from him that her increasing helplessness and her sense of dependence demand, she may react by resenting her pregnancy, feeling perhaps that it has taken away her attractiveness to him. In this case the baby is liable to suffer, after birth if not before.

On the other hand, she may intensify her concentration on the baby, just because she feels that her husband has failed her and is no longer worthy of her love. In this case, too, the baby is likely to suffer. The role of the husband is thus of considerable indirect importance to the welfare of the baby.

Husbands, too, are apt to feel neglected when the inevitable happens and the mother's attention and interest are diverted to the baby that she is carrying in her womb, and they may react in such ways that the tranquillity and contentedness of the mother are disturbed. Thus, even before birth, the baby is entering into personal relationships with his parents, unconscious as he is of the fact.

These possible reactions to pregnancy are given as illustrations of the importance of this period for the child because of the effect they have on the conduct and character of the people who will be most closely associated with him after birth. Other kinds of reaction will readily come to mind. Many of them, like those given, manifest themselves openly, but there are others of an unconscious nature; that is, they belong to the unconscious areas of the minds of the father and mother. These unconscious attitudes, which can never be recognized by the person who holds them, derive from their own infancy. They can play an extremely important part in the upbringing of the child, but I must defer treatment of them to a later point. They are mentioned here because they may be revived by the expectation of a child and may disturb what should be the harmonious unity of husband and wife.

Pregnancy is thus a period in which the parents are getting ready for the birth of their child, in more ways than by preparing his layette and nursery. In the illustrations I have given above of the way in which their attitudes might be affected by the mother's pregnancy, I cited the possibility of resentment in each of them. Usually their feelings are very mixed, and each of them may take attitudes that are contradictory. Resentment in some degree is not unusual, but in the normal course of events it is greatly outweighed by the excited happiness with which the birth is awaited, and by the natural pride of the parents in their achievement. The baby adds a new dimension to their love for each other, and what before had been simply a married couple is transformed into a family. The idea of home takes on a new meaning for them, and they feel personally enriched. They had probably been taught that marriage brings two people into a unity and had striven to realize this, but now the unity is given a living embodiment in their child. Their love and care for each other find a new focusing point, and are thereby made more real. Because she is bearing his child, the husband looks on his wife with awe and an infinite tenderness; while she on her part becomes more aware of her dependence on him, and so feels his strength and masculinity more acutely and turns to him in gratitude that he has fulfilled her womanhood. So the way is prepared for the baby to be born into an environment that will give him the love and care that will be essential to his welfare.

If he is the first child, the greeting he gets will usually be one of love and admiration, shutting out resentment and most of the anxieties associated with birth. If there are other children in the family, the newcomer is certain to meet some hostility and jealousy from them, even if they quickly learn to conceal it from their parents and perhaps even from themselves. The best of treatment by the parents cannot prevent this jealousy, and the right handling of it is one of the delicate problems of parenthood. The older children should not be allowed to feel that the parents' love has been in any measure withdrawn from them because of the new baby; otherwise both will suffer from it. If a real sense of family has been created with them, there is less danger of the natural jealousy taking root and hindering the growth of a sense of sharing: sharing the parents with the new baby and sharing the baby with the parents.

This sense of family is important in another way. The family is the real unit at this stage. A baby should always be thought of in the setting of his family. When he has grown up, his individuality has been achieved, relative to the family, and from one point of view we can interpret growing up as this process of achieving individuality. Even the adult, however, needs to be seen in his relationships, in his social setting. In growing up he has, as it were, extended his family to include all those persons who have in any way had an influence on him and shaped his development.

We need to see the family as the unit for the baby, because this reveals that his helplessness is strength, not weakness. The helplessness of the baby stirs up in his parents the instincts that lead them to protect him and care for him, and these bind the family more closely together. Maternal love and paternal protectiveness are very strong forces. By calling them into action, the baby has strengthened the family and produced new relationships, new orientations in life.

The family turns the helplessness of the baby into strength in another way. Human offspring, if they are to take their place in human society, have to learn far more than is required of the lower animals. Unlike these, as we have seen, they are not equipped by nature with ready-made patterns of action, functioning from birth. Instead, they are endowed with powers of learning far greater than the lower animals have. This learning can come only from experience, granted the innate drives and the necessary abilities. Therefore, it is an advantage not to have fixed ways of behaviour at the beginning, but to be plastic enough to absorb that experience, learn from it, and adapt behaviour accordingly. If the patterns of behaviour had been fixed in detail by nature, they would have to be laboriously undone before benefit could be taken of experience. Hence, the baby is really at an advantage in having to learn almost all his actions. For this, however, he needs his family. Because his parents take care of him over a long period, he does not need to fend for himself and needs a minimum of powers when he is born. He uses the time to acquire his skills, both of body and mind. Compared with the young of animals a new-born baby seems to be at a great disadvantage, but because of his power of learning he very soon outstrips even the most highly developed animals in intelligence and skilled actions.

In the same way his self or personality is only rudimentary at birth. He is a bundle of raw materials of personality, of potentialities for development, which belong together in one body and in the nucleus of a person. Both have to grow. They are only at the starting point of their growth to maturity. Body and mind alike will develop through the experience of living. The raw materials of personality have to be drawn together into the final result of one integrated personal being.

The first few years must be in the setting of a family in which the different members act and react on one another. In the case of deprived children, there needs to be some substitute for the natural family. What the child becomes is limited by his inherited capacities, his native endowment; it also depends on what his family is like, as individuals in themselves and as a social unit in which the baby has to find his place as a member.

CHAPTER 4

BIRTH AND ITS EFFECTS

BIRTH is the first challenge that comes to the baby, and it is probably the most disturbing experience, relative to the strength of his personality, that he will ever have to undergo. It has a profound effect upon him. Strangely enough, this is something that we (parents, teachers, pastors, and so on) can easily overlook, for the obvious reason that he cannot tell us about it. It is not merely true that the new-born baby cannot tell others what being born means to him, cannot describe the pains and pleasures of the experience, the fears and hopes that it may bring; he cannot formulate it to himself in any precise way. Such thinking can be done only by the use of words, and the baby has not yet acquired words to enable his mind to work in this way. Instead of words and the ideas and meanings that they express, his mind can register only the sensations and feelings that are aroused in him by the experience. He has nothing in his mind with which to compare them or by which to identify them, but they are stored in his memory for future use. When he does recollect them, it will be in the form of images and feelings, a reliving of the experience with more or less intensity.

In the same way, this attempt to describe what passes in the mind of a baby must be seen as rationalization and verbalization of the baby's experience. I do not want to be misunderstood in my description of the baby's mind. I am a thinking adult, and when I am trying to form my ideas of a baby's mind, and pass them on to others, I have to put it into words, as though the baby thought it this way. At the best this is only an approximation, intended to drive us back to recover within our own minds, if we can, the experiences we ourselves had in being born. But we cannot recall them. This is not because they happened long ago but because barriers have come down in our minds to stop us having access to the memory of those and other infantile experiences. Part of the barrier is that very process of using words, a facility we all acquire reasonably early in life.

Since we cannot recall our own experiences, and the baby cannot tell us his, it may well be asked how we know what goes on in his mind. Of course, we cannot know for a certainty, however sure we may be that we have understood it, and in any case, as I have emphasized above, we distort it by putting it into words. We are familiar with the various processes of the mind and we can study by observation the developing consciousness of a young child. We know that he cannot use words, so we can infer safely that his brain uses other functions. When, for instance, I touch something hot, my mind becomes aware of the sensation of hotness, a special kind of feeling. In addition, I am very soon able to identify what it is, because I have had other experiences of hotness, although I may make a mistake at first, since intense cold also feels like hotness for a brief period. Further, I am able to give a name to this sensation and to think about the possible consequences of touching something very hot. In other words, I can relate it up to a much wider experience and fit the sensation into a coordinated body of knowledge that I have accumulated. The new-born baby has none of this experience, and therefore can be expected only to become aware of the sensation of hotness. He cannot recognize what it is until he has accumulated several experiences of it, and he certainly cannot name it. The only way in which he can think about it is by the recollection of the sensation itself, that is, by the image of it that is stored in his memory. His first conscious life must therefore consist of the store of such sensations and feelings of pleasure and pain of different kinds which he rapidly builds up. It is easier for adults to think about this in words, put into logical order, but the child must think by linking together the images he has acquired. Mother, for instance, is a complex group of images – the feel of her breast and arms, her warmth, the pleasure she gives him, the sound of her voice, and so on. To the adult, sight and hearing are the most important means of perception, and provide by far the greatest part of the material used by his conscious mind. In the baby, the sense of smell is probably his most significant approach to the world, and after that comes feeling. It is many weeks before he uses his eyes with real effectiveness. His mouth is his most sensitive organ at first, for his survival depends on its activeness.

This gives us some idea of how the new-born baby begins to think. What does he think about? To answer this, we have a number of sources to which we can turn. We can examine objectively what birth does to the baby; we can find traces of babyhood in our own minds; and we can see what seem to be manifestations of it in social and cultural fields, such as religion, poetry, and legend. First let us look briefly at what birth does to the baby. It does three things:

In the first place, it subjects him to what must be his most trying experience, the process of birth itself, whereby the pressures exerted on him by the constriction of his mother's muscles force him through a narrow passage out of the womb and into the world. Fortunately, this is a non-recurring experience. Some births occur more easily than others, but in every case it must have a profound effect upon the baby.

We cannot get direct evidence from the recollection of this experience, for the reasons stated above. The baby cannot put the experience into words. What remains of it in the bottom of the mind can do so only as an image.

Many psychologists claim to have found irrefutable evidence of the persistence of this image, this recollection of an experience, but in other contexts. They say that it recurs in many neuroses and character traits, particularly in those associated with anxiety states. Some even claim that it is the prototype of anxiety. The word 'anxiety' is derived, as Freud pointed out, from a Latin word meaning a narrow passage, and to be born is to be forced through a narrow passage. Most people feel uneasy when they are 'caught in a tight place', but in some this uneasiness swells rapidly into an almost unbearable anxiety and even panic when they are subjected to mental, moral, or social pressures that threaten to constrict their freedom of action. The same root motivation seems to be present in cases of claustrophobia (fear of confined spaces), a very common neurosis. It would appear that memory of the experience of birth, which is latent in the mind, is stirred up by the prospect of having to face some difficult passage or be shut in some enclosed place, physically in the case of claustrophobia, metaphorically in the other cases. The anxiety that is then felt is largely made up of the feelings the baby experienced in being born – constriction of movement, helplessness, breathlessness, and so on. There is much evidence to support this contention.

The second thing birth does to the baby is to bring him out of the shelter of the mother's womb into the world outside, where he has to be a separate physical unit. In the womb he was fed and sheltered from shock and from cold; all was provided for him in an effortless existence. In the world he has to begin to fend for himself and to endure what the world does to him. His first breath shocks him and makes him cry. He is exposed to cold and heat, to pressure and roughness, and other sensations both pleasant and unpleasant. We cannot say how far he had anything like consciousness while still in the womb, but as soon as he is born his mind must begin to function, registering the sensations his body brings to him from inside himself as well as from outside his body. Of course, he has no awareness that he has a body. That piece of knowledge has to be acquired gradually, like knowledge of the world beyond it. All he can know is the pain of breathing, the discomfort of cold, and presently of hunger, and the other sensations his body, now exposed to the world, brings to him through his various organs of sense – the feel of the hands that grip him or of the cot on which he lies, the clothes or blankets in which he is wrapped, the sounds and smells that come to his ears and nose, the sensations of being lifted and set down, all of them new to him, screaming at his newly working brain or consciousness. The very working of his mind must itself be disturbing to his peace.

He cannot be aware of what any of these things mean, for he has had no experience of them and so has nothing in his mind by which to recognize them. Everything at first must be confusion and meaninglessness. It is certain, therefore, that the first impression of the world upon him is one of pain and discomfort and disturbance. Instinctively he tries to escape from it. He cannot get back into his mother's womb, but he would like to recapture its peace. Then things happen without his knowing what they are, and his pains begin to disappear. Breathing ceases to hurt him as his body takes over the automatic control of it. His other needs get cared for, and he sinks back into the unconsciousness of sleep, which is the nearest he can get to a return to the womb.

Pain and turmoil and need return when he wakes, but soon he begins to find pleasant as well as unpleasant sensations, the pleasure of feeding, for instance, or of being bathed or held close to his mother. Gradually he grows accustomed to bearing some of the pains that seemed at first so intolerable. Recognition, and with it pattern and meaning, begin to form, and he starts to find his place in the world.

A third aspect of being born is that severance from the mother's body imposes on the baby the need of putting forth effort. He has not merely to endure what the world brings to him; he has to work to get his satisfactions. His first efforts at work are instinctive and rather rudimentary. He has to breathe, to use his mouth to suck and his lips to grip the nipple by which the food he needs comes to him. If something is troubling him with which he cannot deal, he cries, as an instinctive means of drawing attention to himself, perhaps after he has made spasmodic movements of his limbs and body. These are his first efforts at work. He has to begin to lay hold of the world if he is to go on living. Just as Adam had to earn his bread by the sweat of his brow when he was driven from the Garden of Eden, so, too, has the baby to learn the principle of work, of winning the satisfaction of his needs by striving. The world no longer offers its gifts freely. They have to be wrung from it.

To be born, then, means to learn what hunger and pain and hardship are. It means learning to endure and, more than that, it demands that we put forth effort to help ourselves, to overcome the world that seems to attack us with hurt and cold and noise as soon as we enter it, and turn it from enemy into friend and supporter. This can come only gradually, and the first and inevitable reaction of the baby is to seek to recapture the security and comfort of the womb out of which he has been driven. This is impossible.

From the moment of birth onwards, two forces struggle in the human being. One is the force of growth that drives him forward to face the world and live, to realize that the hurts and hardships it brings are steps on the ladder of life. The other is to retreat from the challenge, to try to escape from its pains and pressures, and above all from its demand to put forth effort, to have to toil to live. On the one hand, acceptance of life; on the other, refusal in whatever way seems possible.

I said a little earlier that we cannot expect anyone to put into words the experiences he undergoes at birth, for the reason that he had no words then in which to formulate them even to himself. The most we can hope to do is to trace the imagery of birth in subsequent experiences that resemble it in some way. One of the clearest illustrations of the way our attitudes are shaped by the pressures of birth is to be found in the eschatology of the various religions, the conceptions they hold of the ultimate state to which we pass beyond this world, the Christian heaven and the corresponding ideas held by the non-Christian religions. The goal of Hinduism is to attain the reabsorption into the undifferentiated ultimate, Brahma, from which we emerged. The world of space and time as we appear to experience it is illusion. We know reality only when we lose our individual consciousness and are merged in the eternal, timeless, neutral infinite. The same denial of the value of individual existence is to be found in Buddhism, in which the perfection of existence is not to exist at all. By learning to give up all desire, all striving, we escape from the weary round of reincarnations to which we are otherwise condemned. What Hinduism and Buddhism are in effect saying is that we attain bliss by reversing the process of birth, giving up the separate individual existence it forced upon us, evading the need to strive and the pains it brings to us, and returning to our mother's womb with its effortless, timeless, undifferentiated mode of being.

The traditional picture of heaven makes it also a symbol of the womb. It is a place where pain and suffering cease (for the blessed, at least), where tears are wiped away, and toil is ended. A thousand hymns delineate this supposedly ideal state. Pain and struggle are our inevitable lot here on earth, but when the Jordan of death is passed we shall enter our Promised Land and receive the reward of our faithful endurance. True, in this picture we do not lose our individuality, but life is made smooth and easy for us, free from the hurts and the hardships we knew first when we were born. So we make our heaven a denial of the worth-whileness of life here on earth, for those are the characteristics of this life. 'Man is born unto trouble, as the sparks fly upward.' Adam must win his bread with the sweat of his brow. Not so in heaven.

I am here concerned only with the psychological significance of the doctrine and not with its theological or scriptural justification. I must, however, point out that it is in conflict with what Jesus meant when he said, 'Ye must be born again.' Rebirth is the door into the Kingdom of God. To be born again does not undo the process of the first birth. It can only mean going through an analogous experience. It implies that the first birth was good, or it could not be used as a metaphor to describe the second birth, by which we become a new man. And far from avoiding pain and suffering, Jesus said that anyone who became his disciple must take up his cross and follow him. As for work and struggle, he said, 'My Father worketh . . . , and I work,' and he constantly enjoined his followers to strive.

It is quite apparent that a false element has crept into our Christianity in the picture of heaven which is so commonly portrayed, even when we do not take the picture too literally. It embodies a yearning to escape the responsibilities that come to us when we are born. That can only be because there persists in most of us at least a deep-seated longing to turn back from life and re-enter our mother's womb. If religion is such a reversal of birth, it is a denial of life. But true Christianity asserts the value of life, and life is what is promised to us by Christ: 'abundant life', both here and hereafter. The new-born baby needs, therefore, to learn to accept what being born brings to him. This he cannot do unaided.

Since the effect of birth on the baby has such profound religious potentialities, we may ask what parents can do to help. In the first place they should not become anxious about it. Birth is a universal experience, like death. What matters is how the experience is used. Something may perhaps be done physically to make birth as easy as possible, not simply for the mother but also for the baby, and this may be the more important. Nothing, however, can make being born anything but a profound shock to the baby, a shock that he has to endure. The aim of parents needs to be to make the endurance of this shock worth while, by the love and the care they give to him from the moment he is born. If the world proves to be a pleasant place, a secure place where the endurance of pain and effort are followed by greater satisfactions such as love and pleasure bring, the baby can soon learn to accept them willingly and not try to run away from them. The severity of birth, if it leads to a rich and happy life, may even thus become a source of moral strength, by showing that by this great effort of endurance the passage was won from a colourless, if tranquil, life to one much fuller of interest and with intensities of joy in it, one much more desirable and satisfying. It is here that the mother can help her newborn baby, and to that we now turn.

CHAPTER 5

MOTHER AND BABY

It is impossible to exaggerate the influence the mother has on the whole growth of the child. The first two years of his life after he is born belong to her. She is almost his entire world. If we are to understand what she means to him, we have to follow all the stages of his growth during those two years. To set the term at two years is somewhat arbitrary, for there is no violent break between this phase and the one that succeeds it, and the period is longer or shorter with different children, depending on the particular inborn nature of each child, the treatment given to him, and other circumstances of his life. Two years may be taken as an approximate guide.

The mother's responsibility may be stated easily enough in general terms. It is to help her child lay hold of life and fulfil the potentialities innate in him. To put it in another way: though he begins his existence completely dependent on her, he gradually grows with her help to become independent of her. This independence should not be taken to mean complete severance from her; it means a change in the relationship that holds them together, for independence is compatible with the closest bonds, the bonds of mutual love and gratitude. Independence is not isolation. The whole period of childhood should be one of changing relationships in which parents and child must play their appropriate parts. If either fails, the growth of the child is impeded.

The parents, being adults, have completed their major development, and their personalities are (or should be) stable and fixed. The young child is immature, growing in body and in mind. The rate of growth of his mind and the intensity of its operations is usually underestimated by the parents, even when they fondly exclaim at the 'cleverness' of their child. In the parent–child relationship, therefore, we have on the one side a relatively unchanging personality and, on the other, one that is developing rapidly through the various stages of mental growth. The mother's, and in due course the father's, treatment of the child has to be adapted to the needs of the child at each stage of his growth. A two-year-old child has needs different from those he had at one year, and the mother has to take these into account if she is to help him fully in his normal growth. She should not ask too much or too little of him. On the whole, she is more likely to be tempted to treat him as mentally younger than he is. Consciously or unconsciously she may strive to keep him as a baby, dependent on her, and so run the risk of 'fixing' him in this stage, unable to grow effectively out of it. As all psychotherapists know, this happens frequently and is the source of much trouble.

When the baby is born, he is at first as completely dependent on his mother as he was in her womb. He is unable to feed himself or do anything for himself except breathe and suck. She must feed him and protect him from cold and hurt and other discomforts, and this dependence lasts for many months. So much is obvious. As his body grows, there comes a time when he needs more solid food and, like the food for the baby's body, the food for his mind also has to change.

We have seen that the process of birth is a painful and demanding experience for the child as well as for the mother, and the new-born baby tends to shrink back from his first contact with the world. If he is to live he must lay hold on that world, and the first way of doing that, after the reflex action of breathing, which seems to be an unconscious action, is by taking the mother's breast and sucking. For the first few days he also has an instinctive tendency to grip with his hands, but this dies away and returns only after a few weeks, when the action seems much more deliberate. His chief organ of contact with the world is his mouth. There is good evidence to indicate that his sense of smell is strong and that the smell of his mother as she prepares to feed him stimulates the sucking reflex into action. Probably, too, the internal stimuli from the body when he is hungry cooperate to make the sucking vigorous. The degree of learning in this activity is minimal. He has inherited the capacity and the urge, as part of the equipment with which nature has endowed him.

Sucking is not merely a physical action concerned only with taking in food. It has its mental side as well. We know that it takes away the uncomfortable feeling of hunger, but this effect is slightly delayed until his stomach begins to get filled and the process of digestion begins. Sucking, however, is pleasant in itself. Pleasure comes from the exercise of the muscles involved in the sucking, but above all from the stimulation of the lips. These are the most sensitive organs of the young baby, and their contact with the mother's breast is a source of sensuous pleasure. Later on, if he is given a rubber teat as a comforter, he may be contented with the pleasure he gets from sucking it without getting any milk from it. To the pleasure from his muscles and his lips may be added the pleasure he gets from the taste and feel of the warm milk in his mouth and the smell of the breast.

These pleasures are natural to him and serve a very useful purpose, for they encourage the activity of sucking, by which alone he can take the food to keep him alive and make him grow. But there is another aspect of sucking that may add pleasure, and certainly promotes interest. The baby is equipped with a mind; that is, with the capacity to register the sensations that come to him through his various organs of sense. While he is sucking, he becomes conscious of the smell of his mother, the feel of her embrace as she holds him, the sound of her voice as she speaks to him, as well as of the various sensations from his own body, his lips and mouth, his stomach, his hands, and so on. These sensations are new to him, a form of experience he probably did not have in the womb. They are added to the experiences of birth, and compensate for their unpleasantness. Because they are pleasant, he is ready to seek them again. They encourage the development of his positive thinking. As some of them are repeated, they stick in his memory, and when they occur again they are recognized.

The next stage of thinking is not merely to recognize the experience when it happens, but to imagine it in advance. The stage after that is to plan to bring about the experience imagined and desired or to avoid one that is disliked.

These stages can be seen developing quite quickly in the behaviour of the baby with respect to particular experiences, especially those connected with feeding and bathing, and he manifests delight at the attentions he receives from his mother. He seems to recognize her and to look for her. The feel of her arms, the sound of her voice or her footsteps, as well as the acts of feeding him, all grow familiar. She is the source of his greatest pleasures, and he shows this by his excitement and delight at her coming.

At this point we must be careful not to read into the baby's mind more than is there and ascribe to him ways of thinking like our own. Attention has already been drawn to the significance of the fact that the baby has no words by which to formulate his thoughts, even to himself. There is another way in which his thinking differs from ours. We have the minds of grown-ups, developed by many years of experience. As far back as we can remember we have thought like this, aware of ourselves as individuals, separate from other people, recognizing people and things as distinct from ourselves. We overlook the fact that we cannot remember back past the age of four or five, except for occasional isolated memories. To get back into our own babyhood would mean having to give up thinking as individuals, and as adults.

The baby's mind differs from that of the adult because the baby has not yet become aware of himself as a distinct individual. He is not conscious of himself as a self. He has not yet acquired enough store of knowledge to be able to make the distinctions required by self-consciousness. Because he cannot separate himself out from the world, he cannot yet distinguish other persons and things, as persons and things, from himself or from one another. For instance, he probably soon recognizes that the feel of contact with his mother's breast differs from the feeling of pleasure in his lips, but he cannot say to himself that the breast is outside himself and the lips are inside. He is simply aware of two elements of a mass or complex of feelings and perceptions. He has not got to the stage of grouping these perceptions into self and not-self, and referring the origin of his experiences to one or the other. That comes at a later point and opens the way to a much wider apprehension of the world.

There is no general agreement among the authorities on the age when this consciousness of selfhood takes place. It may be expected to vary with different children, because it requires a capacity for abstract thinking to formulate the concept, and we know that children differ in their native ability for abstraction. One of the signs by which we may recognize that the child has attained it is the use of the subjective 'I' to describe himself, in place of the objective 'me' or 'baby' or 'John'. This generally happens around the age of two years, which is why I have set the first period, the mother phase, as the first two years.

Undoubtedly the use of 'I' must follow some time after the child has recognized his self-identical individuality, for after coming to the realization of his own selfhood he has to make the further step of ascribing similar selfhood to his mother. This he can do only by projecting his own new awareness into her, imagining himself into her mind and ascribing to her the same kind of feelings and desires that he has come to know as his own. From her use of 'I' to describe herself he then learns how to apply it to himself.

Once he has achieved this recognition of persons, his relationship with his mother enters a new phase, that of self-conscious social relationship. Before that, the onlooker can see that the mother–baby relationship is a social one, but the baby cannot. The mother may treat her baby as a person, and indeed it is important for him that she should, but he has not yet isolated her as a distinct unit in his field of experience.

William James, one of the outstanding figures in the whole history of psychology, said that the world of the baby is 'a great, blooming, buzzing confusion'. He probably erred in using the term 'great', for that implies some recognition of relative size, and it seems unlikely that the baby has yet attained to that. To put more technically what James meant, we should describe the baby's perception of the world as a continuum of sensation in which there are no sharp edges drawn to mark off one thing from another, but all is blurred – sight, sound, smell, and feel – rather like a picture badly out of focus.

Here and there within the continuum a few perceptions are coming into clearer focus because of continual repetition, or because of the emotional interest attaching to them, which leads to more attention being given to them. These are inevitably the experiences which come from his mother's care of him as she feeds, bathes, and dresses him. A group of sensations comes to represent these experiences: the smell of her breast, the feel of her arms, the sound of her voice, and, after a few weeks, the sight of her eyes. This cluster of sensations is the prelude for him of the intense satisfactions he enjoys and of the disappearance of any discomfort he may be feeling from hunger or cold or uncleanness, and he very quickly learns to recognize them.

As the baby grows older, more and more detail is discriminated in his picture of the mother. He learns to distinguish different tones in her voice, different gestures and actions. The field of his recognition widens. But the edges of the picture remain blurred. For instance, he cannot at this stage distinguish his father as another person different from his mother. The experiences that come to him from his father are part of the continuum that surrounds the central mother picture. She is the focus of his total picture, but the rest of it is associated with her. In other words, she is the world to him. He can get to know the world beyond her directly only when he has learned to separate it out from his picture of her, and for this he is not yet ready. Meanwhile, everything that happens to him is thought of by him as in some way connected with the mother who stands at the centre of his total picture. Not merely does she feed him physically and keep him alive; she also provides the food by which his mind grows.

In addition to the need to sustain and develop his body and his mind, the baby has a third need, more persuasive than the others, which for want of a more precise term we may call a spiritual need. If it is not fulfilled, the satisfaction of the other needs can never be fully carried out; for it is only when this third need is fully met that life takes on its proper richness. It is the need to love and be loved. At first the need to be loved outweighs the need to love, for the latter can only get adequate expression when the child has acquired a knowledge of persons. The need of love is basic to human personality. It begins at birth.

We have seen that being born is a painful process in

itself and that it exposes the baby to pain and discomfort and compels him to put forth effort to survive. He would like to return to the untroubled life of the womb, but cannot. The loving attentions he receives soon banish the pain, and the effort he is called on to make brings both satisfaction and pleasure. He has met love and taken the first step in learning that effort brings its rewards. But he grows hungry again, and the pain returns and has to be dealt with all over again. And he learns other pains that come to him by accident or in the ordinary routine of living. His experience is a jumbled one of pleasure and pain, of peace and of disturbance. The fuller his life grows, the greater the variety of pain he meets.

The helpless baby is at the mercy of his pains. He can do almost nothing about them but struggle aimlessly and cry in protest against them. But help comes to him and his troubles disappear for the time being. We have seen that he soon comes to associate his mother with the relief she brings, but we need to take into account that he also refers his suffering to her. She is at the same time both good mother and bad mother.

He does not of course explicitly think in these terms. I am trying to articulate in words the vaguer processes of his thinking. Pleasure he welcomes, and as soon as he learns to desire it consciously he accepts it as part of himself. He resists pain, and it always comes upon him as an enemy, even when the pain is, as we know, from inside his own body. The bad mother to whom the pain is ascribed is therefore an enemy, wishing to destroy him; the good mother is a friend, is part of himself. Since at this stage of his life the child cannot distinguish between himself and his mother, and between his mother and the rest of the world, this is the same as saying that the world is good or the world is bad.

The more helpless the child is, the more important it is that the good should outweigh the bad. When he grows older he can find ways of changing the bad into the good by his own effort, but as a baby this is impossible to him and he is dependent on his mother to make the world a good place for him. Her natural love for him predisposes her to seek to do this. The normal mother is devoted to her child and is ready to make great sacrifices for him, not seeing them as sacrifices but as natural things to do. Maternal love, however, needs to be supplemented by maternal intelligence, and mothers have to learn what are the best ways of expressing their love, that is, by what kind of treatment they can best secure the healthy spiritual as well as bodily development of the baby. Too often it is assumed that maternal instinct untaught prompts the right treatment.

It is true that for the healthy development of the baby unfailing love by his mother, even untutored love, is an indispensable essential. A child that has not met this love is crippled from the beginning and is never at home in the world. All his life he will be seeking it in one form or another. Fortunately, the mothers are rare who do not love their babies. Unfortunately, that love is often in some measure perverted by alien elements masquerading as love – vanity, possessiveness, jealousy, and the like, which spring from the mother's own inadequate spiritual development and of which she may be quite unconscious. Such love is self-centred and feeds upon the child rather than nurtures him, and aims at the emotional pleasure of the mother instead of at the welfare of the child.

A healthy maternal love will produce in the child three things necessary to his growth – a sense of security, ability to face pain and hardship and overcome them by effort, and third, the capacity to love in return. These three are closely interconnected, depending on each other as aspects of the same thing.

For the first few months the baby is too helpless to do much for himself and too immature in mental development to have more than a rudimentary picture of his mother, so that, while he may show great enjoyment of the pleasures she brings him, and while he may eagerly anticipate them, he is not yet ready to give a personal love. His greatest need in this period is for security.

We have seen how the recurrence of hunger and allied pains disturbs the peacefulness of his existence and makes the world feel hostile to him. When this happens he needs reassurance, which comes from his mother's prompt care of him. If she delays in attending to his needs, he grows afraid of the enemy pains that are attacking him, for he is powerless to do anything about them. Then for a time his fear gives way to anger, for fear is always a trigger to release the instinct of aggression, and he is filled with a great desire to destroy his enemy. Once released, his anger lays hold of him.

Young children have not acquired the balances and mutual checks between their instincts that are characteristics of older people. They are subject to what has been called 'the all-or-none reaction'. Their impulses are not released in fine gradations of strength, but are almost without inhibition. Moreover, they can pass from one emotion to another with great rapidity. A child may be laughing one minute and weeping bitterly the next and laughing again in the next minute. The baby feels his aggressive anger with overpowering intensity. It lays hold of him completely. Immediately he feels that he is in the grip of another attacker, for his very aggression threatens to shake him to pieces. He is not aware that it is his own, for he has not yet realized his selfhood. It is like something from without. In consequence, he grows more afraid, and panic supervenes. It is against this kind of suffering that he needs to be secure. The mother provides this security by dealing promptly with his needs.

A baby cries to draw attention to himself. Some cry more readily than others, according to their particular disposition. In any baby prolonged crying is almost certainly the sign that something is wrong with him. It may be digestive troubles, or not enough milk, or it may be an uncomfortable need, too many clothes making him overheated, or something analogous. The mother should try to find out what is the trouble and if possible remedy it. Failure to do so breeds a sense of insecurity in the baby, for he is being attacked by pains against which he is helpless. It also tends to develop in him a sense of being unable to cope with the world; he may begin to be afraid of it and be defeated by it from the beginning. It is cruelty to make a young baby suffer needlessly, even for the sake of some imposed regime of feeding and care. A baby is a growing personality, and the needs of his spirit are of paramount importance.

When a baby has been allowed to suffer unduly, exaggerated expressions of affection are not a compensation for him. He needs the reassurance of loving attention conveyed to him in every way possible, but continued repetition of the sequence, unbearable suffering followed by indigestible affection, may so fix the sharp contrast in him that he will find it difficult to grow into an integration of the two. It may prevent him coming to accept a world in which both pain and pleasure are to be found. He will be in danger of trying to keep them apart and of swinging from one to the other, of seeing the world at one moment as too hard for him and at the next as too easy. As both the good and the bad will be ascribed to his mother, he will have irreconcilable pictures of her, and he will be torn in two by his desire for her and his fear of her. The consequences of this for his religious development we shall presently see. Before we touch on that, we must look at the baby's development in regard to the other aspects mentioned.

In spite of what has been said in the preceding paragraphs, one of the most important contributions the mother can make is to help her baby to endure pain and the frustration of not getting immediate satisfaction of his wants. Life must not be made too easy for him. She must prepare him for the world in which he will have to live out his life. Unless he learns to endure and to strive, it will defeat him, so she does him an ill service if she does not from the beginning encourage him to face his troubles and to make the effort necessary to gain the pleasure he desires. He has to learn that immediate satisfactions are not always possible and that in some cases endurance and effort are the ways to increased satisfaction.

The guiding principle is that the baby should not be expected to bear or do more than he has the capacity to do and that it is with his mother's encouragement, and not in her absence, that he is asked to face the unpleasant. The baby, and later the growing child, should not be given tasks of endurance or work which are clearly beyond his powers, although these should never be underestimated. Moreover, he should not be allowed to feel that by failure he has lost his mother's love. No rules to govern this can be laid down in advance. In each case the mother must be alert to the needs and the capacity of her child. The young baby can do very little, but as he grows in knowledge and strength he can be encouraged to greater efforts. The mother who tries to protect her baby from every possible suffering and to do everything for him is likely to be a bad mother, for she is not fitting him for the demands that will inevitably be made upon him when he has passed his babyhood.

The third aspect of his spiritual growth in this stage is the awakening into activity of his instinct to love, and the shaping and directing of it as it develops. To love actively is just as important to the child's welfare as is the love that should meet him. The first object of his love can only be his mother, for she is the first object he gets to know. Before that, in the early months, his emotion can scarcely be called love. He enjoys feeding at his mother's breast, and the evidence seems to show that that is the first thing he recognizes, and he takes delight in his warm bath and the other signs of care given to him. He learns to like being cuddled and played with and talked to in a happy voice. All these give him pleasure, and he responds with feelings of trust and gratitude. The more his diverse experiences of his mother are woven into a unity, the more his response to her grows into what we mean by love, and he shows more and more his appreciation of her presence as a person, and not just as a source of comfort. Her absence becomes one of the strains to which he is subjected, and the boredom of loneliness may impose a great burden on his powers of endurance.

Perhaps it is only saying the same thing in another way, but it is important to emphasize that the baby needs to be treated as a person in his own right, with all the respect that is due to a person. It is tempting to look upon a young helpless baby as a thing, an 'it', and our tendency to call the baby 'it' reveals this attitude. But it is more than a matter of names. From the beginning the baby has rights by virtue of being born, and these should exact respect and responsibility from others. He is not just a possession of his parents; he is an incipient person soon to be capable of entering into rich social relationships with other people. To treat him as a person from the very beginning helps and encourages him to grow into the fullness of personal being, capable of loving and hating, of fellowship and sacrifice, and of finding unity and integrity within himself.

The unfolding of his love can be upset by insecurity, by neglect, or by over-indulgence. We have seen earlier that he may be the victim of unwise treatment and be exposed to excesses of pain or privation on the one hand and of emotionalism on the other. This leads, I said, to a double picture of the mother in the mind of the baby, a bad mother and a good mother, irreconcilable because each side has been carried too far.

This division makes it difficult to love with confidence. If he reaches out in love towards the good mother and meets the bad mother, the shock to him is all the greater. Not only has his love been frustrated; it has been treacherous, for it led him to suffering. The tendency then is for his love to turn back upon himself, and he will give his love to his own desires and images rather than to the real mother. If, however, her treatment of him has been good and wise, his love for her will grow steadily and be an integrating element in his developing personality. His love for her and his trust in her will help him to undertake tasks she asks of him, tasks from which he would have shrunk had he not this love and trust in her.

We may postpone to a later chapter the consideration of other details – such as the training in bladder and bowel control – in the mother–baby relationship, because the principles that should govern them are the same as those already set out in this chapter, and the novel element in them will come up in respect of other developments. We may pass instead to the meaning of this period for the later religious life of the individual.

It is not and cannot be itself religious on the part of the baby. The mother's attitude towards him will be influenced by her religious outlook, but I do not propose to say anything about that, as her proper attitude should emerge as we go on with the study of the child's development. Although the baby has no religion, this period with the mother lays a foundation, possibly the most important foundation, for his future religious life.

In this period the baby begins to make his own contacts with the world, after the sheltered life in the womb. His mother is the world to him. He must first get to know her, and can only pass through her to the world beyond. Until he is about two years of age she is the focus of all his experience, and therefore the world takes its character for him from his experience of her. We can lay down the fundamental principle that unless he learns from her what love is and learns in turn to love her, he is going to find it difficult, if not impossible, to understand later on that God is Love. In the measure that he builds a picture of the mother as bad, he will later see God as an enemy. If he develops a sense of insecurity, God will always appear to him arbitrary and unpredictable, now stern and cruel, now over-indulgent and willing to overlook any misdemeanour. He will fear God and he will try to cajole him.

On the other hand, if he has met the right kind of wise love from his mother, he will face the world with trust and confidence, even when it hurts him, for he will have learned from his experience with his mother that beyond the pain and the effort of work demanded of him there lies an even greater satisfaction. He will go on in faith that if he endures and trusts, there is goodness to be found. It will not be a stoical endurance by which he will live, for, just as his mother asked patience and effort from him, so he will see that God asks the same at a more advanced level, and he will know that he is not suffering and called on to toil because God's love has been withdrawn from him, but that these may be the very signs of God's love. His mother's love has been a preparation for him to understand the character of God. She has in fact been mediating God's love to him.

CHAPTER 6

FATHER AND CHILD

BEFORE the baby is many months old, he gives indications in his behaviour of recognizing his father. This of course is to be expected, because in the usual family the father shows most interest, next to the mother, in the baby. The baby's recognition of his father does not mean that he sees the father as a person. All that we can assume is that the experiences he derives from his father's handling of him form a cluster of perceptions that tend to have a unity in themselves, with its own recurring pattern of pleasure, pain, and mental stimulation. This father pattern should be seen as a subsidiary focus of interest within the general all-embracing pattern of the mother. The father is an attachment to the mother, and no doubt some of the emotions the baby feels about the mother also flow over to the father when he is present to the baby.

As the young child grows, and his experience is accumulated and his mental powers developed, he forms many such subsidiary patterns. He gets to recognize other children in the family and the familiar objects, toys and so on, that surround him and form part of his everyday life. His perambulator, his cot, his chair are all familiar to him. He learns to group sounds into patterns of meaning and to make some of them himself in speech. His own body has become a well-defined object with qualities different from other things in his environment, so that he can produce sensations at will by putting his toe or his finger in his mouth and by touching the things around him. His mind is expanding at an incredible rate.

About the age of two years a crisis of development takes place. The general pattern of which the mother has been the chief focus, giving her character to everything else, begins to break up into its constituent parts. The subsidiary patterns begin to take on their own independent existence. The initial step is the separation of the baby from his mother, his realization of his own selfhood, followed very quickly by the understanding that she, too, is a person with ideas and feelings like those he knows in himself. He has become capable of self-consciousness. A new kind of world has opened to him. From now on, he knows his own solitariness. He is shut up in his own mind and knows himself over against the world. He knows himself also as part of the world. He can perceive it and think about it, but he can be aware of himself thinking about it. He is both subject and object to himself, but all other things and persons are only objects. Of course, the full realization of this comes only gradually, and indeed it remains true of most people that they never attain to full objectivity of outlook, but, in some areas of thought at least, mistake subjective convictions for objective fact.

The advent of self-consciousness, with its division of the world into subjective and objective, involves another process affecting the whole future outlook of the child and his relations with the world. It has to do with his emotional attachments. Before the division he drew no distinction between his perceptions of the world and the world itself, for distinction had no meaning before he became self-conscious. After the division he can distinguish between the image in his own mind and the reality to which it refers. The question then arises: will his emotions be directed primarily to the real object or to the image of the object? According to the way his emotions are attached, he will be what Jung has called extravert or introvert respectively. (I should add here that this is not Jung's explanation of the genesis of these two types, whose existence is generally recognized. For practical purposes

I accept Jung's classification, but not his general theory of types.)

The extravert is easily at home in the world. His emotions flow out freely to people and things and he joins spontaneously in whatever is going on around him. He puts people at ease and promotes social feeling. On the other hand, he is not much given to reflection and introspection, and even his feelings do not run deep for very long. The introvert finds it difficult to display his feelings, yet they may be deep and enduring. He is introspective and has to feel his way into the world by his thinking. Instead of acting directly upon the world as the extravert does, the introvert first constructs a mental image of it and uses this as a kind of map to find his way about. The extravert is likely to excel in action, the introvert in thinking. The extravert has to find his way to the knowledge of himself and of God through the world; the introvert finds his way to the world and God through himself.

Most people are a mixture of the two, but the extremes I have described here are common enough. Whichever attitude appears in the child will colour the whole of his subsequent development.

How far the particular disposition of any individual is innate to his constitution cannot be known with any great degree of certainty, but it is reasonable to suppose that the experience of excessive emotional strains in the mother period may have some effect in turning the child towards introversion, by making him somewhat afraid of the world. His disappointments and frustrations have in that case driven him to a stronger attachment to the image of the perfect mother than to the actual mother. He then attains to love of his mother by projecting on to her the image of the ideal mother in his mind. This identification of the ideal with the real is an unconscious act, never the result of deliberate intention.

The tendency to invest images with strong emotion is

active in respect of the father and is perhaps the chief formative factor in the child's development in the years from two to five. In these years the foundations of the child's future religion are taking shape, and in this and the next chapter we shall try to see the pattern that is being formed. Needless to say, it is a very intricate one, and opens up infinite possibilities of variation.

We have seen that the baby's early recognition of his father does not imply recognition of him as a separate person, but sets him within the all-inclusive mother idea. Once the child has achieved self-consciousness and discovered himself as a person over against his mother, the way is cleared for extending the concept to his father. The difference, however, is vital. The child by this leap in abstraction sorts the mother out from himself. His mother is somehow part of himself. He has to detach the cluster of experiences that represent the father from the mother after she has been separated from himself. It would seem, further, that the father pattern takes over other subsidiary patterns that have in turn to be sorted out from it. This sorting-out process can be illustrated by a child of my acquaintance, who, after coming to distinguish his father from his mother, addressed all other men as 'Daddy'. He soon passed to the next phase, in which he called only his father 'Daddy' and the other men came to be 'Mr X' (the name of his father's closest associate). Bit by bit he learned to recognize more and more people as separate individuals. This illustrates the way the area of our clear knowledge is gradually extended.

Because the father is separated out from the objective mother and not from himself, he is always *other* to the child, always something of a stranger and an alien to him. This sense of 'otherness' is reinforced in the child by his relations with the father in the next few years. We shall have to follow these in some detail to see how the transition is made, but at this point we can anticipate the conclusion and say that our conception of the person of God is a development of the young child's conception of his father. One of the popular descriptions of God is that he is 'wholly other'. We can see the reason for this in the way the child first realizes his father as a separate person. For a well-developed religion, that infantile image has to be metamorphosed, and not simply projected on to the idea of God; but the young child has not developed far enough to be able to achieve the metamorphosis, and any attempt to graft the idea of God on to this first image of the father is disastrous for his future religious growth. He needs first to work his way through to a stable relation with his father.

There is another important difference between the child's knowledge of his father and that of his mother. His first knowledge of his mother was in a dual relationship with all the intimacy of belonging to each other. His knowledge of his father as a person is in a triangular relationship – father, mother, and self – which immediately begins to introduce cross-currents of emotion. In it there cannot be the same unquestioned intimacy with the father as there was with the mother, and even the relations with the mother begin to be disturbed by the new development. The child's life has suddenly become complex, and he has to learn to become a social being and to find a solution to the conflicts that are set up inside himself, for in the triangular situation jealousy and fear spring up, as well as love.

At this point the boy and the girl begin to diverge in their development. At first the divergence is not very great, but by the age of five years they have taken different lines of growth so mutually exclusive in some respects that the mind and personality of a man is different in kind from that of a woman. They think differently and have a different approach to moral questions. Of course, there is much they have in common, and most people have a mixture of masculine and feminine in them, which obscures the basic difference, but to ignore it is to land in misunderstanding. We can illustrate this simply. The first love object of both the boy and the girl baby is the mother. Out of that primary love the other loves develop. The girl begins her love life with a homosexual love, the boy with a heterosexual. When the father appears on the scene, the dominant heterosexual trend of sexual instincts makes it easier for the girl to effect the transition to love for him, whereas the boy will remain longer in his attachment to his mother and will take up mixed attitudes to his father – love and admiration mingled with jealousy and fear.

From this point onwards, therefore, we need to discriminate between the sexes, for the description of the boy's development does not fit that of the girl, even though there need not be very great difference in the treatment given them by their parents, in that both need the security of love and encouragement. I am therefore faced with the problem of exposition. Logically, I suppose, there should be two books, one for the girl, the other for the boy. That may be going too far. Instead I shall follow the growth of the boy as the main theme, breaking oft from time to time to sketch in the picture for the girl. This may be unsatisfactory for some, but I can plead only that more study has been given to the masculine line, and therefore more is known about it, and further, since I am a man, I possibly have more insight into the masculine side.

The boy first sees his father as a second mother. This is to be expected because he has separated him out from the primary picture of the mother, and in addition the behaviour of the father is akin to that of the mother, for father plays with him, talks to him with the same sort of caressing voice, nurses him, and may at times help in feeding him and bathing him.

Long before he became recognized as an individual on his own, he was familiar to the child and loved by him.

This love continues, but two new emotions grow up alongside it that lead to an altered attitude to the father. The two grow up in parallel lines, as it were, and while they may interrupt each other they do not blend. They are admiration and jealousy.

The boy sees his father as a godlike creature, knowing everything, able to do everything. He is big and powerful and seems to come and go as he pleases. Even the wonderful mother seems to defer to him, to attend to his wishes and to recognize his power. (The boy at this age has no idea of the meaning of authority, but can think of it only in terms of power.) She prepares the meals for him; she eats with him at table rather than with the boy himself; and no matter what the boy does to capture her attention and compel her into his service, he does not succeed in breaking the father's hold over the mother.

Clearly, he sees, the father is the source of security, so he turns to him for the protection that he feels he needs, even though he may seek consolation for hurts from his mother. The boy learns that when he grows up he, too, will be a man like his father, and his parents encourage him in this by urging him to 'be a man' when he has to bear something painful or undertake some task he finds hard. So he forms an idea of himself on the model of what he understands his father to be. He *identifies* himself with his father.

Let us look a little more closely at this process of identification. The term is used in psychology as a technical one to describe a phenomenon of behaviour that is in my opinion the chief means of mental and spiritual growth, as well as a powerful bond to hold society together. We can compare and contrast it with imitation.

We frequently imitate other people because we admire them. Children make a regular practice of it. We try to be like our heroes, so we imitate their bearing, their speech, their mannerisms, and the like. Such imitation is deliberate, and we know what we are doing, even if sometimes we are a little ashamed to admit it openly. We are copying what we perceive of the other person's behaviour. In identification we also behave as the other person does, but there is no deliberate intent to do so and no conscious effort is made to that end. Usually we love and admire the person we thus copy, but we may hate and fear him. The point about identification is that in it we unconsciously see an identity between ourselves and the other person, and we behave as if we were that person without knowing that we are doing so. Unconsciously we live in him, we become his person for the time being, and as a result we take on his characteristics. Imitation we can carry out as an act of will, but identification is out of reach of will power. It lies much more in the sphere of the imagination and the emotions, at the deep levels of the personality. It may be only a one-way link, but it can be two-way.

Identification should be distinguished on the other side from delusion, of which we see typical examples in certain types of mental illness. A paranoiac, for instance, may positively assert that he is the President of the United States. So far as we can see, he unquestionably believes that he is, and for the time being has no recognition of his own real identity. It is a confusion of identities from which he is suffering. In identification there is no such confusion. If the boy identifies himself with his father, he does not believe that he is the father; he knows that they are two separate persons. He may not even know that he is behaving like his father, though here it is hard to draw a line, because admiration, which leads to imitation, usually goes hand in hand with identification.

The area of the personality involved in the identification may be extensive, so that almost the whole is affected, or it may be limited to a single strand; and the same is true of the manifestations of identification. Similarly, the identification may be transitory or it may be enduring, and the links that promote identification may be of the slightest character or may represent a wide community of interest. Whatever the form it takes, insofar as one person identifies himself with another he takes on for the time being the character that is the keynote of the identification. If the identification has a deep personal significance for him, the assumed characteristic – mode of behaviour, mannerism, mental outlook – is likely to become a permanent modification of his personality. To such an extent can this happen that husbands and wives frequently grow like each other because they have mutually identified themselves with the other. The highest developments in the religious life come through identification. The Christian identifies himself with Christ and takes on his character – if the identification is real – and in the last resort adoration of God implies an identification with God, or perhaps leads to it.

To return to the boy and his father. The boy loves, admires, imitates him, and then identifies himself with him. But he sees his father from his own point of view and with what limited abilities and interests he has developed. He does not see his father as another adult would see him, or with the correcting perspective that greater experience would give him. Indeed, one of his first tasks after the seven years I have given to infancy is to adjust his picture of his father to more realistic and objective lines. His infantile picture is highly exaggerated. He sees him as infinitely great and wise and powerful, having no limits to his grandeur. Boys of much older years will be regularly heard to boast, 'My father can do anything.' Because of the helplessness of the boy compared with his father, the picture is also invested with strong emotional tones. This image of the father thus formed in the boy's mind becomes significant in its later evolution as the first model of the idea of God.

The other major element that enters the father image formed by the boy is of a negative character. He becomes aware of his father's individuality in the threefold situation of father, mother, and child; never in isolation from the mother. He soon begins to take account of the relations between the other two. Up to now he has been unaware of any challenge to his full possession of his mother. Children are naturally egocentric. They cannot be anything else until they get a considerable knowledge of other persons and make extensive identifications with them. The young boy therefore takes it for granted that his mother will attend to his wishes, and he assumes without question that this is what she exists for and what she herself desires to do. Now he becomes aware that she gives considerable attention to the father, attentions that frequently conflict with what he wants and compel him to take second place. He grows jealous of his father. He wants him out of the way so that the old undisturbed relation with his mother may be restored.

When he tries to understand why the mother attends to the father rather than to him, he can come only to the conclusion that the father exercises some compulsion over her. His assumption that she is his prevents him imagining, at this early stage at any rate, that the mother might really wish to serve the father and that the father has prior claims on her love and her attention. So the father takes on an aspect of cruelty, and very soon the boy, who wants to get the father out of the way, begins to imagine that his father feels the same about him. The father is so enormously powerful to the boy's mind that he is irresistible, and the boy feels that he is in danger of being destroyed by his father. One of his fantasies at this stage is that his father will eat him up. In the ancient Greek myths Chronos devoured his children. And fairy stories like Jack the Giant Killer are loved because they do not sound improbable to little children. The giant eats up little boys, but the hero outwits him and slays him instead. That is what the boy wants to do to his father.

The average father and mother looking on their little son may not suspect the existence of fantasies such as these in his mind and may be tempted to think that I am describing children already depraved. I assure them there is ample evidence that what I am describing is part, but only part, of normal development, and in the next couple of chapters we shall see that this negative attitude to the father has an important part to play in driving the boy forward to an adult point of view. Without it he would remain in perpetual infancy, permanently attached like an infant to his mother.

It is only in later stages of development that the boy achieves some synthesis of the two streams. Meanwhile, his jealousy and fear exist in a parallel stream of feeling with his admiration and love of his father. There is a further complication. Because he loves his father he feels some jealousy towards his mother. This is not so strong, because his love for his father is not so fundamental to his being as is his love for his mother.

As the boy comes towards the end of his fourth year, his emotions grow more defined and stronger, and the conflict between his love for his mother and the fear of his father becomes so unbearable that he has to find a way to escape. That we shall turn to in the next chapter. To end this one, we should take a brief glance at the development of the girl.

Like the boy, the young girl carries forward into the father phase her early love for her mother, but her subsequent development follows a different line. Like the boy, she begins to see her father as a rival for her mother's love and to be jealous of him. This does not develop to the same pitch of intensity as it does in the boy because she soon turns to the father as a love object. This is prompted by two things. In the first place there seems to be a strong heterosexual bias in our sexual instincts, and this in the girl leads her to transfer her love to the father more easily than does the boy. Second, this is reinforced by the inevitable difference in the behaviour of the parents, who are also governed by heterosexuality. They treat their children differently according to the sex of the child.

The mother will see her son as a little man, a reproduction of her husband, and behind that will probably lie an unconscious image of her father. She will see her daughter as a reproduction of herself, and the love she gives to her will be less tinged with direct sexual overtones. It will be of the character which psychologists call 'narcissistic'. She will see herself beginning again in her daughter. Similarly, the father will take pride in his son as a second edition of himself, and see his daughter as a reproduction of his wife. Again, behind that there will be almost certainly an unconscious image of his mother.

This diversity of emotional interest on the side of the parents helps to produce corresponding reactions in the child. In the case of the boy it strengthens his attachment to his mother. In the case of the girl it takes her over from her mother to her father. As a consequence, the girl does not develop fear of the father to the same extent that the boy does. This becomes extremely important in the next stage of development.

The young girl soon becomes aware of her femininity. She does not picture herself as growing up to be a man like her father, but a woman like her mother. In saying this, I am aware of the disappointment held by many girls that they are not boys, and of their efforts to behave like boys. This is a point to take up later. In general, little girls are encouraged to take their mothers as their examples, and their nature prompts them to do so. They tend to identify themselves with their mothers as boys do with their fathers. This in turn increases the girl's femininity.

The identification with the mother differentiates the development of the girl from that of the boy in two ways. Towards the end of this period, that is, soon after the age of three, children become interested in discovering where babies come from. Sometimes they get straight information from their parents and learn that a baby is first nourished inside his mother's body. If they are rebuked or given false information, they may begin to think that this is a forbidden or shameful topic, and repress their curiosity. Their silence on it is no proof that they are not eager to know. The normal healthy child needs the information. He learns directly or indirectly that babies are always born from women, not from men, so the little girl who sees herself becoming a woman like her mother builds fantasies of herself having a baby. This is encouraged by the dolls that she is given. She transfers her fantasies to them and uses them to strengthen the ideal of herself. She plays herself, as it were, into the role of the mother. With that she takes on the attitude of dependency that seems to be the mother's role in relation to the father.

The second difference from the boy comes from the common recognition of the father as the head of the family, that is, as seen from the young child's point of view. The girl, like the boy, sees the power of the father over the mother and builds up a picture of him as all-powerful and all-wise and as the protector of the family, the provider of good things. She has not the same motive as the boy for fearing this power, because the transference of her love to him from the mother reduces her jealousy of him. She grows jealous of her mother instead and she wants her father to give her the baby she expects as a woman to have. If this hope happens to be over-strong, the inevitable disappointment of it may lead to resentment against the father for letting her down, but in the usual course of events the father image formed by the girl is not such a conflicting one as that formed by the boy.

The consequences of this will be apparent in the next chapter.

The relevance of the father phase for the religious development of the child is immediately apparent when we recollect that all religions tend to think of God as Father, and Christianity in particular specifically enjoins us to pray to him as such. Not only children but adults are taught the Lord's Prayer, 'Our Father, which art in heaven . . .'

In what sense do we mean the title? As adults we explain it as an analogy or a metaphor, but quite obviously we first find a meaning in it from our experience of earthly fathers. The sophisticated theological argument that we learn what earthly fatherhood means from the Fatherhood of God is a misleading one. The truth in it is that when we have extended the idea of fatherhood from fathers in the flesh to God, we have brought new meanings into it from our experience of God, and these new meanings can be brought back to apply to our fathers in the flesh. This is a secondary step. The first step is to apply to God the ideas of fatherhood we have learned beforehand.

If a young child is taught that God is Father, he cannot avoid applying to him the ideas he has formed of his own father, the ideas I have been describing in this chapter. These ideas belong to the very immature outlook of the young boy or girl. They are quite inaccurate as a realistic description of the father as other adults see him or as the child will see him after the lapse of sixteen years or so, or even after six more years.

It may be objected that the child will grow out of such infantile ideas of God. The answer to that is that a great many people do not grow out of such ideas about their parents, but bury the infantile images in their unconscious minds, where they exert a powerful influence on our outlook and behaviour. It is far easier to grow out of ideas about our real parents, as we shall later see, than to outgrow infantile ideas about God. One has only to read a few well-known hymns and prayers to see how they embody infantile ideas about God. If again it is argued that these are the kinds of ideas about God that we ought to hold, the answer then is that religion is a matter for infants and not for full-grown men and women.

We must not give up the contention that religion has a place in mature personalities. For this, it has to be a mature religion based on the strength of personality, not one grafted on its weakness and immaturity. The father phase is only the beginning of the child's understanding of his father. Until that is completed the child cannot grasp the real significance of the Fatherhood of God.

CHAPTER 7

THE CRISIS OF INFANCY

THE human mind is the most complex thing that we know. However far we may penetrate into its mysteries, it is doubtful whether we can ever hope to understand the fullness of its functioning. The task of exploring it is made more difficult by the infinite variation between individuals. When it is the minds of young children we are trying to understand, there is a further obstacle, the fact that in certain ways their minds work differently from those of adults.

We have already noted some of the differences in an earlier chapter. A further one is that young children have not developed very far the ability to distinguish between fantasy and reality. This ability comes only as the result of accumulated experience in dealing with the world and by the gradual testing of what is real and objective and what is wholly fanciful. This is a slow process, and many adults continue to blur the distinction in some areas of their thinking, particularly where personal interest is involved or strong emotions are evoked. Nevertheless, adults have developed a sense of reality, even when it functions imperfectly, and for all the practical purposes of life they regard the distinction between what is real and what is imaginary as essential to make.

Another important difference between the mind of a young child and that of an adult is that the child has not yet developed a function of the mind that all normal adults have and cannot put aside. It is only developed at the end of infancy, by processes that we must examine in this chapter. It is the screening or censorship function that operates in all adult thinking. Because of it, adults' recollections of their own childhood are unreliable, as has been demonstrated in countless experiments and clinical examinations, and most of the experiences of infancy are driven out of memory altogether. The same function distorts their observation of young children, especially of their own. The study of young children is a very specialized pursuit, and those who take it up have to overcome the difficulties imposed by their own inner mental censor, which operates for the most part unconsciously, as well as to make allowance for the other differences to which attention has been drawn.

Some of the findings that have emerged from the modern study of the development of children seem horrifying and even unbelievable to the ordinary parent. They seem to show little children as monsters of depravity. That is because the ordinary parent does not make the necessary allowances for the differences between infantile and adult minds, but unreflectingly assumes that the child thinks and feels in the same way as he or she does. Certainly if an adult entertained the same ideas and desires that are to be found in little children, they might well be thought depraved.

Children do not yet possess the standards and the inner coordination of mind that mark the adult, and they therefore indulge freely in fantasies the adult rigorously suppresses in himself, so rigorously that he is usually not aware of entertaining them. But what would be depravity in adults is normal in little children. All children have to pass through this stage as part of their growth. If older children turn out to be delinquent, this is not to be explained by their having these tendencies in early childhood. It is due to their not growing through them, that is, to getting fixed in them. When we rightly call little children 'innocent', we do not mean that they think only good thoughts, but that they cannot distinguish between right and wrong, in a moral sense, and that they do not deliberately intend the wrong things they do. I do not mean by this that children are not sometimes deliberately 'naughty', that is, they do things they know are against the wishes or commands of their parents. Children are frequently naughty in this sense, but this is a way of testing the love of their parents and not the fruit of an evil disposition. If children are constantly naughty, the parents should not suspect their child of being incipiently depraved, but they should look to themselves first. Their treatment of the child is probably the cause of its misbehaviour. This in turn may spring from their failure to understand the problems with which the child is wrestling.

Any effort such as this book is making to expound some of these problems suffers from two disabilities. For the sake of clarity it is advisable to follow up each thread separately, as far as that is possible. Since the child is advancing along all lines at once, that gives a false impression and oversimplifies the picture of the whole child. Divergent or contradictory strands of development can be going on at the same time in the young child. They do not cancel each other out, but they can influence each other as part of the process of growing up. No one particular strand represents the child. He must be seen as the confused total of all of them, and the picture he presents can change with kaleidoscopic rapidity. It is very difficult, therefore, to give a simple description of his progress or to avoid apparent overemphasis of some tendencies at the cost of others.

The second disability of exposition is that any description of the various stages of development is bound to foreshorten them and make them appear sudden, whereas in actual fact the movement from one stage to another is always gradual and with a considerable degree of overlapping, so that it is impossible to say with definiteness that one stage has ended and the next begun. I have tried to make it clear that the ages I have assigned for the different stages are not to be taken absolutely. They are only rough guiding marks, a warning to be on the watch for the next stage.

I have thought it advisable to make these preliminary remarks before going on to deal with the next phase of the child's development, because that phase is one of the most complex and because it is one that most people find difficult to grasp and believe. It represents the crisis of early childhood and brings babyhood or infancy (in the psychological sense) to an end. Freud was the first to recognize its profound significance and to draw attention to its real character. He called it the period of the Oedipus complex and its passing. This is a useful name, for it vividly depicts the nature of the central struggle in the child's mind. In the ancient Greek story, Oedipus mistook his foster parents for his actual parents and unknowingly slew his real father and married his mother. Translated into the forms of infantile desires, this is what the young child wants to do. It is a defect in the use of the name, however, that it thrusts the masculine side too much into the forefront and does not take sufficient account of the development of the girl.

Nothing else in Freud's teaching has been so bitterly attacked as his description of the Oedipus complex in children as a normal phase of development. It is true that the original statement of it requires some qualifications, and indeed it has been modified. It is true also that the very controversy over it has thrown it out of proportion and obscured the other aspects of development in this phase, with the consequence that psychoanalysts sometimes seem to ignore the social and personal influences bearing on the child and concentrate too much on the sexual. Nevertheless, to use an old simile, to expound the development of the child without taking account of the Oedipus complex is like trying to give Shakespeare's *Hamlet* without the Prince of Denmark. And it is ironical that many who reject the idea of the Oedipus complex readily use concepts that are derived from it, 'inferiority complex', 'mother fixation', 'father substitute', and so on. So far as we can, let us forget the controversies and try to look at what is going on in the child's mind.

In the last chapter we saw that increasing knowledge of the father results in the genesis of conflicting tendencies in both boys and girls, but of a somewhat different character. These come to a crisis in the period we are about to consider. The crisis is partly produced by the normal development of the sex instincts of the child, which now begin to move towards the adult forms. It is therefore necessary to review the main outlines of the functioning of sex in children.

This is a difficult subject to talk about, for three reasons. In the first place, it is a very complex subject, requiring a whole book in itself, and any brief account of it, such as this must necessarily be, inevitably is liable to be misleading, if only because of oversimplification. I am well aware of that danger, and, if what I say appears dogmatic, I ask your forbearance. I am more concerned to go on to show how these developments are related to the religious growth of the child than to prove their correctness. To go into proofs would take us too far afield.

The second difficulty comes from the fact that we all have reticences and mental barriers that tend to make any open discussion of sex somewhat embarrassing and that hinder us both in our thinking about the subject and even in our observation of facts. These mental barriers are both conscious and unconscious. We can train ourselves to talk objectively about sex by overcoming the conscious hesitations we have about discussing sex, but it takes a long time and much painful effort at self-knowledge before we can overcome the unconscious barriers. As these barriers are mostly erected in the stage of development we are now considering, it is precisely about the sexual developments of this stage that we are most blind and have the greatest resistances.

We are helped if we can find our way through the third difficulty, which is that of terminology. Freud's effort to solve this difficulty failed. He brought in the term 'libido' to denote the energy of the sex instincts, but it has proved to be too closely associated with the ordinary meaning of 'sexual' to achieve the result that is necessary, that is, to give us the comprehensive picture of the growth of the sexual instincts. When we think of sex we almost invariably do so in terms of adult sexual impulses and activities. We know sex as a powerful impulse – some would say the most powerful – that motivates large areas of human life. It drives a man and a woman to desire union with each other, union of bodies, union of personalities, of interests, the complete sharing of life. Around the central core, the urge to coition of bodies, and related to it in various ways, are many activities of a physical, emotional, and spiritual character. These include simple caresses, courting, display in many forms, home building, and a host of other ways in which love normally manifests itself. They also include the many forms of sexual perversion, which are so named because they are unmistakably derivatives of the sex instinct. All these ideas, feelings, impulses, actions, form the background that the word 'sex' evokes in our minds and give it the meaning it normally has for us.

We get a different picture from the objective study of the development of the sexual instincts. The capacity for full sexual activity does not develop until after puberty, but its roots have been present long before that. The evidence for this is overwhelming. Sex does not begin just at puberty. The adult forms of sex are developments out of more diffuse forms, which are active right from birth. There is a continuity of development; therefore the sex instincts (for we should more properly speak in the plural) need to be interpreted over the whole range of their functioning and not simply as they express themselves in adult life.

If we interpret the word 'sex' simply to mean the phenomena that show themselves in adulthood, we are narrowing its meaning and making it difficult to see the inner relation between the many ways in which sex develops. Most of the cultural activities of man, including his religion, draw their energies from the roots of the sexual instincts, but to understand how this happens we have to realize that the genital and reproductive activity of sex in the adult is only one of the developments out of the infantile forms. Adult sexuality, profound and powerful as it may be, is a canalization of more diffuse impulses in the young child. It is misleading to think of sexuality in young children simply in terms of meanings derived from adult forms of expression; but it is an even graver error to overlook the diversity of the manifestations of the sexual instincts from infancy onwards.

We ought to recognize this the more readily if we consider the wide use to which the word 'love' is put. Love is primarily an emotion or sentiment roused by the activity of the sex instincts, but behind every form of love there is a corresponding development of these instincts. We speak of being 'in love' when the whole range of sexual (in the adult sense) desires is directed towards one person, but we also speak of such things as love of food, of music, of truth, of freedom, of home, of friends, of country, and so on. Ordinarily we would not think of these as sexual objects, and in the adult sense of the word they are not; but such 'loves' are derivatives from the basic sex instincts, even the love of God, and we cannot understand the development of a human being unless we understand how this comes about.

The first manifestations of sex in babies are not genital at all, and therefore usually are not recognized for what they are. They take the form of sensitive zones whose stimulation gives pleasure. For the first few months the baby's mouth is his (or her) chief organ of pleasure. He satisfies his hunger by sucking, but the action of sucking, with its stimulation of the lips and of the mouth muscles, gives its own delight. Thus his mother is at the same time a hunger object and a sex object, that is, a source of merely sensory pleasure, and the baby is bound to her by both forms of satisfaction. The same sensitivity to stimulation seems to be diffused over the whole body of the baby, but with less intensity than there is in the lips. Some months later, when teeth are coming, biting gives the same kind of sensuous pleasure. Later still, in the second year, the processes of evacuation of the bowels and bladder give an intense pleasure and become a matter of great interest to the baby. They also provide a means of showing love to the mother and of winning her love in return.

I shall not attempt to describe all the forms of infantile sexuality. They are important in the formation of character and need to be taken into account as causative factors in deviations from normal development. The main point that I wish to establish here is that there is a sexual attitude to the mother on the part of the infant, growing from birth, and that this can be strong, even though the forms that it takes and the satisfactions that it gives are not those of adult sexuality. The young child gets an intense pleasure from the caresses given to him by his mother and from the attentions she gives to him in her daily care of him. The baby is 'in love' with his (or her) mother. The love grows with the growth in the child's capacity to feel and to express himself in more and more ways. It is not weakened when the father is discovered, as described in the previous chapter. Its very strength leads to the crisis of infancy to which I have referred and which must now be explained more fully.

At about the age of three and a half years, at a rough approximation, the child – boy or girl – passes into the phallic stage, as it is called. In this period the main sexual sensitivity (or sensuous pleasure) of the child has moved to the genital organs. One sign of this is the tendency, so frequently observed, and so embarrassing to parents, that children of this age have of playing with their genitals. It is called the phallic stage because both boy and girl take the norm of development to be the *phallus*, or male organs. If the little girl has discovered that she is not like a boy (and from seeing babies or other children almost all do), she imagines that in due course she will grow organs like his.

In the phallic stage there is an intensification and localization of sexual feeling, which begins to approximate more to the adult form, and at the same time there is a great enrichment of the fantasy life. A little reflection shows the reason for the latter. In the earlier phases the desire for sensuous pleasure got its satisfaction from contact with the mother in feeding or in her attentions to bodily needs, or in the processes of evacuation that could be offered as a gift to her. In the new phase there is no obvious way of getting the physical satisfaction, as there had been in the earlier. The sexual tension therefore builds up and then gets its main release in fantasies, not in physical form. The fantasies are not the result of the childish masturbation, but are more probably its cause. Because the mother is still the chief love object, the fantasies centre upon her and picture some form of genital contact with her.

This separation of the sexual life into two main streams before sex has reached its full adult form is an essential step in the development of the child. One stream, that connected with the bodily organs, goes forward to take its final shape in adult sexuality and its complex of sentiments and activities. The other stream, seeking its satisfaction in a rich mental life, leads away step by step from the sensual modes of pleasure to modes that are so far removed from the primitive roots as scarcely to be recognizable as sexual. The energy of this stream flows over into the intellectual and cultural pursuits that begin to develop, among them being religion.

The division into separate lines of development is consolidated by what the phallic stage leads to. The intensified longing for the mother brings the child up against the father, so he imagines, and into a crisis of emotional conflict. This crisis has to be resolved in the course of the next two or three years. The way taken by the boy differs from that of the girl, so we must consider them separately.

The young boy, as we saw in the previous chapter, sees his father under two aspects, good and bad, friend or enemy. As the good father he is protector, able to do everything, knowing everything, the great ideal to be admired and loved, the pattern of what he himself wants to become and, because he is a boy, will become. At the same time he sees his father as his rival for possession and control of the mother, and with the increase of his desire for his mother in the phallic stage, the rival becomes for him an enemy. He wishes that his father were out of the way so that his love relation with his mother could go on undisturbed. He inevitably projects similar desires on to his father; that is, he imagines that his father feels the same hostility towards him. Because his father is so big and powerful, the boy feels helpless against him. He longs for some way of overcoming his father. This is the pattern of the fantasies that are expressed in all the fairy stories and nursery tales in which the young hero fights and overcomes giants and ogres and rescues the beautiful damsel. The more he loves his mother, the greater the danger he feels from his father.

The young boy is thus caught between the fire of two strong forces. On the one side is his love for his mother, which has been the meaning of life to him up to now and into which all his energies have poured. On the other is the fear of his father as the all-powerful rival for the mother. The boy imagines that if he persists in his love for his mother the father will destroy him in some way, or, what is tantamount to the same thing, destroy his power to love his mother. The more he loves his mother, the more he fears the 'bad' father. The dilemma would be insoluble but for the 'good' father image, which he now calls to his aid. The 'good' father is all that he aspires to become, his ideal. He identifies himself in this aspect with his father, and the desire to be his father thus becomes a powerful motive in him.

By taking this image of the father into himself, he adopts the father's point of view as his own, and the father-in-himself now gives the orders that in his fear of the father he had imagined the latter was giving to him, namely, to give up his desire to possess his mother sexually – as he understands sex. The introjected father, that is, the father as taken into himself by identification, now gives the orders, and that means that the boy gives the orders to himself, for by the introjection one part of him has now become the father. The introjected father image forbids him to go on loving the mother in this sensual way. This reinforces his actual fear of what the father may do to him, and he gains control over his desires. He is enabled to renounce his sexual desires for his mother. When the renunciation is completed, his desire for her is transformed into tender emotion or simple affection, in place of the sensuous excitement and pleasure he had hitherto sought from her. He is no longer in danger from the father. He has chosen the way of obedience to save himself. He has passed through the crisis of infancy.

Two important results follow from this crisis. The first is that the boy's love is detached from his mother so that he is able to seek other sexual objects and love them for themselves, not just as repetitions of the mother. This is the condition for a successful married life later on in adulthood. The crisis of infancy is a necessary stage to set a boy free from his mother. Without it he would be permanently attached to her.

The second consequence is that there is a permanent alteration in the boy's mind. The internalized image of the father becomes a regular part of the structure of his mind, a kind of overself, a *superego*, as it is called. Because of the way in which it was formed, the superego exercises authority within the mind, supervising every desire and every thought that rises in it (not only the sexual, although these are most subjected to censorship), and it forbids those that are contrary to the commands it seeks to impose upon the behaviour of the boy.

Before the formation of the superego, the behaviour of the boy was controlled by fear of the consequences – loss of the mother's love or punishment by the father – and by hope of reward. Now there is an internal standard to judge everything and to give orders. The boy has become his own authority; that is, he has become capable of judging himself, and does judge himself by means of his superego, and is always under internal pressure to obey the standards set. He is now a moral being. He has passed out of the age of innocence and henceforth must answer to himself for his conduct, and not simply to his parents or to others having authority over him. His superego now gives him a sense of right and wrong. As the superego takes more and more rules of conduct into itself, so will his moral education progress.

The progress of the girl follows a different line. Like the boy, the girl has the mother as her first love object. When the father is perceived as a separate person, somewhere after she reaches two years of age, the normal heterosexual bias of the sex instincts leads her to take him as a love object. She still goes on loving her mother, but not so intensely as does the boy, in whom the heterosexual bias strengthens his attachment to his mother. In the girl there are two competing loves and therefore two rivalries as well, more evenly balanced than they are in the boy. She is jealous both of father and of mother. The intensification of love in the phallic period and its separation from physical satisfaction, noted above, bring the crisis in her also to an unbearable pitch. Although her love, and her jealousy, are divided between the two parents, it would seem that her fears are mainly concentrated on the image of the father, because he has come to be seen as the source of authority in the family.

Three factors make her way of solving the crisis different from that of the boy. We have already drawn attention to the first, that her positive attitude to the father is one of love, rather than of admiration, which is the boy's attitude. The girl oscillates between fear and love of her father.

Second, her feminine role has been emphasized to her by word, by dress, by toys, as well as by the emotional attitudes taken to her by her parents and others in the family circle. All the social pressures that bear on her, conscious and unconscious, push her to identify herself with her mother, not, as the boy does, with his father. Since she has come to believe that the mother is subservient to the father's authority in the family, she therefore accepts with the feminine role the same subservience to authority.

The third factor is the anatomical and biological counterpart of the second. The girl has to come to terms with the difference of sexual function between male and female. Up to this point there is no significant difference in the development of the sexual instincts of boys and girls. The girl now has to take a further step. She has to renounce the impulses of the phallic stage and accept the fact that she will not grow organs like a boy. This at first may make her feel deficient and inferior.

The little girl is enabled to make the necessary transition to the feminine role by her identification with her mother. She has just discovered, unless she has been stupidly misled, that babies grow in their mothers' bodies and that only mothers can have babies. She, therefore, being a girl, a small edition of her mother, can look forward to having a baby. Since a boy cannot, this is her compensation for not being like a boy. It is perhaps, even more, a ground of superiority. Her temporary sense of incompleteness is made good to her in the knowledge that she can have a baby. It was some deep intuition of this that led St Paul to say that the woman 'shall be saved [that is "made whole"] through the childbearing' (I Timothy, 2:15).

I should say in passing that the development I have just been describing is the way of normal growth for the girl. Instances are common enough of girls who resist femininity and strive to be boys and who rail at the restrictions and slights that are put upon the feminine sex. Those who take this attitude refuse to give up the phallic stage and its fantasies and to accept the compensating power of childbearing. They want to remain and prove themselves masculine. I venture to suggest that the proper transition out of the phallic stage to true femininity is helped by giving children, boys and girls, straightforward information when they ask about the source of babies. Interest in this question is one of the marks of this period, and factual answers in simple form should be given to their questions. The knowledge that babies come from the mother is of vital importance for the girl in helping her out of her crisis.

It will be noticed that the path taken by the girl in resolving the crisis of infancy does not involve her in introjecting the authority of the father, as the boy has to do. She therefore does not acquire a superego like that of the boy. He takes obedience into himself as a way of escaping the threat to his power to love. She accepts the sacrifice of her masculinity and regains the power to love through her body, her femininity, her baby that is to be. The boy henceforth is governed by the internal authority of his superego; the girl measures life by its promise of creativeness, corresponding to her newly understood power to bear a baby. Since the superego is the seat of the moral conscience, this means that girls develop a different kind of conscience from that of boys, and a different approach to moral problems. They have different senses of right and wrong, not chiefly because of differing education, or failure of education, nor only because of social pressures, but because it is normal for them to grow in that way.

Once the girl has crossed the bridge to the acceptance of her feminine role, she begins to prepare herself psychologically for the baby she is to have. She looks to her father, not as the source of authority and the ideal to follow, as does the boy, but as the giver of babies. For the girl that means the giver of life and the restorer of love. She wants to be loved by him, for that enables her to love in return. She is made whole again by being loved.

It is obvious that this difference in the development of the two sexes has enormous significance for ordinary life. It bears deeply upon religion, too, for the image of the father is the first stepping-stone on the way to the understanding of God. Already here at the age of five or six the way is laid down for different approaches to God. It would be foolish to claim that one way is better than the other. There is no common standard by which to judge. We can only accept the fact of their difference. In their final development they meet in a common ideal. God is the goal of masculine aspiration; he fulfils womanhood also by his love.

This difference of development is almost certainly part of the explanation of the commonly accepted fact that women come more easily and in greater numbers to religion than do men. Their approach is more direct and personal and they can more easily understand a personal God and a God who is love. There is less fear of God in women, just as the young girl has less fear of her father. It does not mean that women are more religious than men; it means only that the barriers to be overcome in growing towards God are not so difficult for them as for men, because of the way they have developed. This is not the only explanation, but it is an important contributory factor. It emphasizes that our God must be a God of love as well as of righteousness.

CHAPTER 8

INFANTILE AGGRESSIVENESS AND ITS AFTERMATH

THE account of the infant's development given in the previous chapters has of necessity been simplified, keeping only to the main lines of growth and leaving out secondary developments and deviations from the normal. In a subsequent chapter something will be said about the effect of fixations, that is, failure to grow completely through any given stage and so to be unable to pass on to the next. There is, however, one aspect of development that we must now consider, because it supplements what was said in the previous chapter about the formation of the super-ego. It is the place of aggressiveness in the growth of the child's mind.

Apart from a brief reference to the rages of a baby in Chapter 5, we have been considering the development of the sex instincts, their forms of activity, and the attachments and transformations they undergo. Aggression, however, plays a large part in shaping the personality that is being formed by the growth of the child.

The aggressive instincts are part of the natural endowment of the child, along with the self-preservative and sexual instincts. Their function is to cause their possessor to attack an outside object, physically, or in any way possible. Clearly they can serve a useful purpose. In their crudest and most direct form they impel the individual to defend himself in moments of danger by attacking the enemy that threatens. Even the mildest of men or animals is likely to turn when cornered and fight desperately. But the action of aggression is not confined to physical violence. It can take an infinite variety of forms, subtle or obvious. It can also link up with the other instincts, love and self-preservation, and help to further their purposes.

In its most positive aspects it is a drive within the personality to lay hold on the world and win from it the fulfilment of desire and of need. In this way a baby's aggression helps him to seize his mother's breast and endeavour to swallow it. Aggressiveness can be used in a constructive way whenever it is duly subordinated to other ends, for in all construction there must be some destruction. A house cannot be built without shaping each piece of material to fit in its place; weeds must be uprooted and the ground dug to make a beautiful garden; to make a dress one must cut up the cloth; and every child soon learns that in his play he must destroy the materials he uses – make marks on the lovely clean paper, alter the shape of the clay or modelling material he is using, knock down one sandheap to build another, pour out the water to make mud pies, and so on.

In these ways aggression is useful. It becomes a danger to the self and to society when it is not duly subordinated to other ends but instead breaks loose and becomes an end in itself, when destruction and anger and hatred give satisfaction for their own sake. They are more dangerous when the satisfaction they give is disguised as pleasure in the fulfilment of some other purpose, while unconsciously the sheer lust of aggression has been the true motive, even though it may be unconsciously so.

We all know the great pleasure we get when on some occasion we are allowed to indulge freely in our aggressiveness and destructiveness for legitimate purposes: chop down a tree, like Gladstone, smash up and burn some old piece of furniture, set off a pile of fireworks, and so on. Children, particularly boys, seem to pass through a period when aggressiveness and destructiveness are their main interests, when they fight for the pleasure of it, and every pane of glass is a temptation to stone throwing. One grown-up child once said that his idea of heaven was an infinite number of glass houses with convenient heaps of stones to be used on them! And slapstick comedy always makes a great appeal to children, because they can enjoy vicariously the aggressiveness in it, aggressiveness that is permitted and therefore not to be feared.

In a world in which we live under the shadow of the possibility of complete destruction by the armaments we have devised, in which rival gangs fight in the city streets, and political, national, and race hatreds are to be found everywhere, it is all too clear that aggression is a most powerful factor in human life and that it has broken loose. Its handling presents one of the greatest problems, if not the greatest, that religion has to face. Our mistake in religion, as in politics, is to think that we can handle it from outside, that what is needed is controls placed upon it. The greatest need is to ensure its proper integration into the growing personality and thereby to prevent it passing into purely destructive lines of action.

Aggression is a natural instinct. It is probable that some people are constitutionally endowed with more aggressiveness than others, but this is a supposition that cannot be taken as proved. It has to be confessed that we do not know a great deal about its inner workings. Those who appear aggressive beyond the ordinary, and many do, may behave in this way for some unconscious reason connected with their past experience, and not simply because they were born with a stronger instinct of aggression.

It is a trigger instinct; that is, it comes into operation as the result of something else. The chief activating causes that arouse aggressive impulses are frustration and fear. Aggression may also be released in anyone who believes that he is threatened with attack of some kind, as well as by an actual attack, but this may be thought of as a fear situation.

In some social situations an individual may be roused

to active aggression on behalf of a loved object or cause, or someone with whom he has identified himself, even when there is no direct threat to himself. The greatest degree of aggressiveness is probably that shown by mobs, who on occasion, for no apparent reason whatsoever, will indulge in orgies of uncontrolled destructiveness. The behaviour of mobs bears irrefutable evidence of the strength of our aggressive impulses, for in mobs the normal self-control exercised by an individual is lifted and the instinct is given free play, so that we see what it can do.

It is impossible to avoid occasions of frustration in young children. The baby does not always get his hunger satisfied at once; or some pain that is afflicting him cannot be removed quickly. When he is a little older and has toys, one of them gets lost and cannot be found in spite of his demand for it, or he wants to have the lighted candle to play with and is not allowed to. Or his mother is unavoidably absent when he wants her and calls for her. Later still, he may resent the arrival of another baby and want it to be got rid of; and in any case he wants at times to have his father out of the way so that he can go on enjoying his mother's love undisturbed. Some of his desires can never be satisfied; others may have to wait a long time.

This is unavoidable. But it is not harmful on that account. One of the most important lessons that he has to learn, for the sake of his own development as well as the need to fit into the family situation, is how to bear frustration, temporarily in some cases, totally in others. He has to be helped to learn this, and that means that he should not be subjected to frustrations which are really unnecessary, through lack of foresight or indifference to his welfare, nor should he be called on to bear frustrations beyond his strength, where this is avoidable.

If he has to be denied something that he wants, a substitute for it should be found, so that he gets some satisfaction. If he is continually subjected to frustration of his desires and does not get enough compensatory satisfactions, this may well lead to much aggressiveness being released in him which he is unable to absorb into the service of other activities. It will remain as pure aggressiveness and, even though it may get repressed into unconsciousness, it will find ways of expressing itself in hatred and destruction.

There is one consequence of infantile aggression that is of particular interest. Aggression is in the first place a defence provided by nature against enemies that threaten to destroy us. But if it is violently aroused, his own aggression can appear as an enemy to the baby. The young child has not built up checks and controls on his impulses, so if he is frustrated for long his aggression may be released in full force, and its very violence threaten to shake him to pieces. Anyone who has seen a thoroughly enraged baby knows how his anger can get a grip of him. The baby, of course, does not know that it is his own anger. All he can know is that something has reduced him to helplessness, and this has become a new enemy.

When he has become a little more aware of his surroundings, though not yet self-conscious, at the age of a few months, he is possessed by a great desire to swallow his mother's breast, which to him is the source of all his delights. His aggressiveness towards the breast then threatens the object of his love, and he grows afraid of it and tries to deal with it. Dr Melanie Klein has made some fascinating studies of this phase of childhood.

When his aggression thus becomes so powerful that it threatens to overmaster him, the young child deals with it by becoming aggressive towards it, or rather, towards the manifestations of it, treating it as an enemy. The effect of this is to split his aggression, one half turning in upon the other in the attempt to banish it. Frequent repetition builds up an enduring centre of self-directed aggression that watches over his 'dangerous' impulses, that is, his outwardly directed aggressive ones. A division or conflict is introduced into his developing self.

This division of the self, it must be emphasized, is to deal with situations that appear to the child as dangerous. At this early stage he has no conception of right and wrong. That only comes after the resolution of the Oedipus complex. When that occurs and the image of the father is introjected to become an internal authority enforcing standards of conduct, the superego thus formed inherits the power of the earlier self-directed aggression. This is to be expected, for the Oedipus complex is a danger situation – involving the fear of being destroyed by the father – and it is only by passing through it that the child is transformed into a moral being capable of making moral judgements.

It may easily happen that a baby is provoked to great outbursts of aggression requiring the development of equally strong counter-aggression. The helplessness of the young child to defend himself or to take other measures to control his aggression can result in his self-directed aggression becoming abnormally strong in relation to the rest of his personality. This can happen, for instance, from the frustration resulting from difficulties in feeding, a common enough occurrence both with breast and bottle feeding.

The striking paradox then appears that when the self-directed aggression that develops is added to the superego formed out of the resolution of the Oedipus complex, the latter is made abnormally strong, corresponding to the abnormal strength of the self-directed aggression of babyhood; and the particular individual emerges with an overpowering conscience, making moral judgements not because he has high ideals but because of the difficulties in feeding he had as a baby. Feeding difficulties are only one of many seemingly irrelevant causes of developing a harsh conscience. This is a warning to us not to identify conscience with religion blindly. It certainly indicates the need of laying the right foundations for religion in infancy.

The problem of handling aggression is of extreme importance for religion in another way. Over-developed self-aggression lies at the heart of our sense of sin, our feeling of guilt, and of the need for expiation of guilt. Self-directed aggression takes the form of self-condemnation. When the aggression becomes embodied in the superego and takes on a moral tone, the self-condemnation is both an accusation and an admission of wickedness; of sin, when the source of righteousness is believed to be God. It is quite healthy that there should be some self-directed aggression in the form of self-criticism (I am now thinking in terms of maturer people, older children and adults, and not of infants), but the self-condemnation is apt to be carried to extremes, out of proportion to the actualities of the case. It is made worse by the repression into the unconscious mind of the original reasons for self-directed aggression. The result of such attacks upon the self is to drive the original dangerous impulses underground in the mind, where they remain out of the reach of consciousness.

One of the functions of the superego is to keep the most disturbing of our impulses in the unconscious mind, and the process of our repressing them is itself also unconscious. (The difference between *repression* and *self-control* should be carefully noted. Repression is always unconsciously carried out, and therefore we are unaware of what we repress; self-control is a deliberate act in which we are well aware of the impulses we are suppressing.) Because of repression the real grounds of our self-condemnation remain unconscious, but the violence that was attached to it can be transferred, without recognition that it is transferred, to some new act of wrongdoing. This may be worthy of severe condemnation, or it may only be some minor peccadillo, in which case the self-condemnation and sense of guilt are out of all reasonable proportion.

The emotion belonging to self-condemnation is mixed. One response is to feel guilt. Because of the amount of unconscious self-directed aggression we all carry, we have a great deal of guilt feeling. This is frequently also kept in the unconscious, but large amounts of it may escape and become attached to the minor sins we commit and the mistakes we make. Every pastor, and every psychotherapist, knows how heavy is the burden of guilt that people carry, so heavy in fact that a great many people break down from it, or at best are rendered ineffective in the ordinary responsibilities of life. They cannot trust themselves, so strong is their self-condemnation. It is a major task to handle this guilt. Simply to bring the feeling of it out into the open means stronger self-condemnation, which in turn results in an increased sense of guilt, which provokes further self-condemnation. It becomes a vicious circle in which we spend all our energies in confessing ourselves miserable sinners, and have not the strength or initiative to undertake anything else. This is often mistaken for religion, and, indeed, much religious teaching is directed to producing this state of self-condemnation as something to be desired.

The truth is that there is some emotional satisfaction in it. The act of self-condemnation is two-fold, condemnation *of* the self *by* the self. In being condemned, the self feels guilty; in condemning, the self feels virtuous. The sense of virtue is increased when the guiltiness is acknowledged, so confession comes to be an end in itself instead of what it should be, an honest and factual avowal of what one is, as a step towards amendment of life.

This plunges us right into the heart of religion and once more bears witness to the importance of laying the right foundations for it in early childhood. The same witness is borne by another struggle through which the young child must go, the reconciling of love and aggression. This is a life-long task, but it begins at the start of life.

We are endowed by nature with aggression and with love. The one destroys; the other builds up. For a very little while we are allowed to indulge them separately and so at full strength, but the inexorable law of growth lays hold of us and very soon we are struggling to find a way of bringing them together. The ideal is that aggression should always serve love, that we never attack or destroy for the pleasure it gives us, but only to build. Nor should we delude ourselves about our motives, and cherish unconscious pleasure and excitement while we deceive ourselves into thinking that what we do is done for 'good' reasons. Virtue is not a substitute for love, and when we try to justify our aggression on the grounds of virtue alone, we should look for the unconscious satisfaction it is giving us.

All manner of combinations between love and aggression are to be found. A few people find the perfect blend. Some people are able to combine them in limited spheres of their lives, like the surgeon who destroys to cure, or the cabinet-maker who cuts up his timber to make beautiful pieces of furniture, loving the wood he is working upon. Most of us live our lives in separate compartments, allowing love to dominate in some and aggression in the others. Or we swing rapidly from one mood to the other, as sometimes happens in families between husband and wife or brothers and sisters. All the time we are under pressure to reconcile the two. This fundamental need is expressed in the religious ideas of atonement and expiation and the hope of its final attainment in the Christian doctrine of resurrection, by which death, the ultimate destroyer, is finally overcome and disappears.

The psychologist draws attention to the child's need to make reparation for his aggressiveness. Reparation is a powerful innate need of the child. In the baby, not yet conscious of self, it is chiefly shown in his need for reassurance after some outburst of temper. He needs the security of knowing that he is in a world where love is dominant and that his destructive rage has not destroyed the source from which love came to him, his mother. The petting and comforting he receives helps to abate his fear and to strengthen the working of love in him. It is probable, too, that his fondling of his mother's breast just before or during his feed is partly due to his delight that it still exists, that he has not swallowed it in his aggressive attack upon it.

When he is a little older and has become familiar with toys and other objects, he is apt to be greatly upset if any are broken or lost, and it is a reassurance to him if broken things can be mended, for it teaches him that destruction is not final. When he has gained enough courage he takes great interest in dropping things at table or out of his perambulator, for the sake of having them restored to him. Again, this is a test on his part whether love that restores is able to overcome the aggression that destroys and takes away. When he is a little older still, he will prove to himself that he can knock down his pile of sand or building blocks and build them up again.

To understand what is going on in the child's mind, we need to remember that he is not yet capable of drawing clear distinctions between what is fantasy and what is real. The wish to destroy is tantamount to the act of destruction itself. He is constantly afraid of his own aggressions, but just as constantly trying to undo them. Some of the acts of aggression or destructiveness for which parents condemn their children are part of an experiment on the child's part to see if he can defeat his own aggressiveness, or to verify whether there is enough love outside himself to overcome it for him. It is therefore a serious mistake for parents (and especially the mother) to call their children 'bad' or 'naughty'. This confirms him in his fear that he is really bad, that his love is not strong enough to overcome his aggressiveness, and that he has destroyed the love he needs from his mother. Babies and older children want to be lovable and they greatly need all the help they can get to overcome the aggression inside themselves.

The young child's need of parents whose love is unshaken and to whom he can turn for help in overcoming his sense of unlovableness is repeated in the adult's need for a God whose love is unfailing, a God who, in the face of wrongdoing, shows his love by reaching out to help the sinner find the way back (or forward!) to wholeness of life. Salvation means wholeness or healthiness, and religion is concerned with the ways of attaining to such completeness of self. As in the young child this can be done only by the wise help of the parents, so in the adult it can be done only by God. The parents are preparing their child for the later recognition of the meaning of God.

In the later years of infancy children can be helped to be more and more constructive, particularly by toys and games in which they can work off their aggression and at the same time learn to make things. They need plenty of raw materials, not delicate or expensive toys that easily break down and upon which or into which the children themselves have put no constructive effort. In the same way stories in which damage and destruction are undone help their imagination to put the emphasis on the power of love to triumph. The happy ending belongs as much to childhood as to adulthood.

The basic need of the child is not to have his aggressiveness eliminated, for that is impossible and attempts to suppress it are liable simply to drive it underground into the unconscious, but to integrate it in the growing personality so that when he emerges into the world it may be a source of power to him, a servant and not a master, a strength and not a handicap.

CHAPTER 9

EMERGENCE FROM INFANCY

THERE are four major phases in the growth to adulthood: infancy, childhood, adolescence, adulthood. The periods of transition are five to seven years of age, twelve to fourteen, and eighteen to twenty-one. These are subject to variation with individuals; to some extent with education and social environment, and perhaps also with climate and race. The peculiar feature about these phases is that mentally, and especially emotionally, there is a greater similarity between infancy and adolescence and between childhood and adulthood than between any pair of successive stages. It is almost as if the child emerges from infancy into a first adulthood, then reverts to a second form of infancy to emerge from that into adulthood proper. Other animals grow up in a straight line; man seems to grow up twice. This gives the time necessary for the full development of the powers of mind and the rich complexity of personality that distinguish man from the lower animals. To be most fruitful, the education given at each stage should be adapted to the inner needs of the child at that stage.

When the young boy or girl has successfully negotiated the Oedipus complex and thus passed the crisis of infancy, he emerges into the period of childhood, the years from about six to thirteen. There is a period of transition in which the emotional disturbances of late infancy settle down and the new attitudes of childhood expand and grow strong. This transitional period is relatively brief in the case of the boy, lasting from about five to seven years of age. In the case of the girl it is much more drawn out and gradual, and any end we put to it is purely arbitrary.

In childhood the progress made in infancy is consolidated and expanded.

In going through these changes the child is in the grip of the law of growth that was discussed in Chapter 2. He does not have to be taught to grow up; the inner law of his being drives him forward. He needs help to grow, especially at the difficult places. The transition from infancy to childhood is one of the most difficult. It is like being born again. The infant passes into a new world, because he now sees it through the eyes of his newly acquired moral sense, which has added a fresh dimension to his understanding.

Once again we may recall the story of Adam and Eve. They were driven from the Garden of Eden because they ate of the fruit of the tree of the knowledge of good and evil. The moral sense that the infant has developed makes him aware of the difference between good and evil, and he, too, is driven out of the garden of innocence, and cannot go back, however much he may try. Of course, the standards by which he judges are rudimentary and have to be educated, and it is like being born again because it is a turning away from the family to the world, just as in birth he left his mother's body to enter the world.

By resolving the Oedipus complex the young child has renounced the attachments to his parents, particularly that to the mother. As we have seen, it is not easy to do, and the mother herself, if she does not realize what is happening, may try to restrain the development. She is reluctant to let her baby go; she wants to keep him a baby, dependent on herself. Just as there are the pains of physical birth, there are also the pains of emotional birth, which the mother must harden herself to endure. To refuse to give birth to her child in this metaphorical way is to risk killing the personality coming to birth. The period of infancy has been a preparation, a time of mental and emotional gestation.

In turning away from his mother the child turns to the world, and for the next half dozen years his main emotional and intellectual interest will be directed towards it, dispersed over all the fascinating experiences it has to offer. He becomes, as that great child psychologist Dr Susan Isaacs used to describe it, the young scientist. He gets absorbed in finding out about the world, what is in it, and how everything works. He rapidly becomes a realist, eager to distinguish fantasy and make-believe from what is 'true' or 'real'. This happens more quickly in the boy than in the girl, and he turns away from fairy stories to trains and cars and aeroplanes, to rockets, spaceships, and other gadgetry.

The transition to objectivity is not so easy for him in relation to other people, children or adults, who inevitably make a considerable impact on his life, but it goes on gradually. He will study them and note all the oddities of their behaviour with a detailed observation that constantly surprises adults. The latter have sorted their ideas into a system of priorities of importance or relevance, but to the child everything is interesting and therefore important, like the fragments of junk that the boy carries round in his pockets.

As well as observing the people around him, he has to enter into social relations with them. In particular he has to reassess his parents. The images he formed of them in infancy no longer fit them. He is beginning to see them as human beings. In place of the emotional dependence that marked his understanding of them in infancy he now approaches them more objectively and realistically.

The image of perfect beauty, of ministering love, the source of all delights, gradually fades from his mind as the representation of his mother, and he begins to find fault with her. She has the annoying habit of disturbing his play – so important to him because he was just working out some line of thought or making some new discovery –

simply to get him in to meals or to run a message for her. And she is overfussy about washing of hands and neck, and about tidiness, and about the way he ruins his clothes. He begins to compare her with other women, and though he goes on loving her – even when he is a little embarrassed at showing it – he gets her down bit by bit to the level of an ordinary human being.

The same process goes on with his father, who before had been the godlike, omniscient, omnipotent being, to be admired and feared alike. He finds that his father has limitations, that there are many things he does not know or cannot do, that he can be tricked, like mother, by a bit of flattery or cajolery into doing what the child wants. Before very many years are past, the child will be openly criticizing his (or her) parents, telling them how to improve themselves, what their behaviour in such and such circumstances ought to be, and so on, until he is convinced that they are hopelessly old-fashioned and behind the times.

I said that the idealized infantile images of the parents fade from the mind of the child. More strictly speaking, they become detached from the parents, fade from the forefront of the mind, and sink into the unconscious area. For a while they may show their continued existence only as a vague awareness of some perfect being or perfect state to be discovered. From the unconscious, however, they tend to be projected out on to each fresh hero or heroine that the growing child begins to worship. With the first adolescent love they come out in force, and the perfection and beauty and wonderfulness that the infant saw in his mother or father, as the case may be, are seen again in the beloved. The image once more gets in the way of objectivity. The parent images also form the basis of the child's grasp of any religious experience he may receive. We shall take that point up in the next section of this book.

The child has also to learn to adjust himself to other

children. For boys this is the gang stage, in which they tend to link themselves up with other boys in groups, with intense loyalties and rivalries, testing themselves out against the others and finding their level of personal capacity in the gang. Girls do not tend to form gangs in the same way, but appear to look for 'soul mates', best friends with whom to share confidences. It is harder for the girl to break away from the family, because of the way she has to deal with the Oedipus complex, but the possession of a best friend is a great help to her in this, for she can identify herself with the friend and through her find her way out of the family circle and into the world beyond.

The period of childhood, then, is a period of great activity, mental and physical alike, directed outwards upon the world of people and things. The emotional conflicts of infancy have been reduced, and childhood is a time of emotional stability. It is ended only when the natural anatomical and physiological changes of puberty bring about a renewal of sexual development, with a fresh access of energy that brings on new emotional urges that have to be dealt with.

By the end of infancy, however, the foundations of the personality have been laid. What building is constructed on them depends on many things – on the native endowment of the individual, the circumstances of his life, the way he is treated by parents and teachers and others who come in contact with him, the teaching he receives, the opportunities available, and so on. If the foundation is strong, whatever is built upon it will be firm. A bad foundation may lead to collapse of the building. This is true of religion as of any other activity. To that we may now turn.

PART 2

Building Religion

CHAPTER 10

THE EARLY YEARS: THE ORIGINS OF GUILT FEELING

In the first half of the book we have been considering what goes on in the mind of the child as he or she develops through the various stages of growth in the first seven years of life. We turn now to consider more explicitly what parents and educators, pastors and counsellors can do to promote the development in the child of a healthy religious outlook. Let us take stock of the situation so that we may see clearly what we want to do and how best to achieve it.

What is it that we want to do? The words and phrases we commonly use can easily mislead us. We speak of 'teaching the child religion', 'training the child', or 'bringing up the child' in religion. We slip into the attitude that we can *give* the child religion, that the way to make him religious lies in inculcating a set of ideas and beliefs about God, the Scriptures, and the Church; or in getting him to conform to certain rules of conduct and obey the accepted moral maxims; or in forming in him the habit and taste of participating in the forms of worship customary among believers – going to church, saying his prayers, and so on. All these unquestionably may have a great value for the child, as we shall see at a later point, but that value is not necessarily religious, particularly in the young child.

It is true that religion expresses itself in a set of beliefs and a great concern for truth; that it also carries with it the acceptance of principles of conduct; and that it leads the believer to express (and cultivate) his religion by public and private worship. But all these are derivative; they are the ways in which religion expresses itself. Religion is primarily a matter of the spirit, that is, the shape of the personality. This is determined by the interrelations of its constituent parts, the ideas, emotions, sentiments, ideals, standards held, and above all by the drives of the personality that are based on the great instinctive dispositions.

In other words, religion is not just a veneer to enclose and hide the raw material of the personality underneath, imposed upon it by the techniques of education and cemented by the forces of persuasion and discipline; it is the way the raw material itself is shaped and polished into the appropriate forms. We are not dealing, however, with inert material like wood, but with living and growing forces; so the aim of religious education, so called, must be to foster the right growth. We must aim at long-term results, not at quick returns. The processes of growth cannot be hurried without serious risk of doing permanent damage to the personality and preventing the child from attaining the inner strength that is the mark of sound religion.

The aim of religious education, then, is not to constrain the child to become religious, but to ensure that as he comes to maturity of development he will find in religion the fullest expression of his inward self. We must not assume without question that the best way to achieve this is to train the child from the beginning in the forms of religion – prayer, Bible stories, children's services, and so on. The child may find a great interest in all these, but his interest will be of a social, intellectual, and aesthetic character, not religious.

This does not mean that such activities are necessarily valueless as a training for religion or in other ways; they can be very valuable. It means that we must assess them for what they are to the child. That is why it is so important to understand what is going on in the mind of the child, and to adapt our education to the stages of his development. We are constantly in danger of falling into the error of a young mother who came to her doctor to ask advice about the weaning of her baby. He explained to her the kind of food that she might give to him, including a little meat. 'But,' he added, 'you must increase the amounts very gradually.' Two weeks later she came back to him. 'Doctor,' she said, 'he ate two large sausages for lunch yesterday; what do I now give him?' Some people are too ready to rush their children on to large spiritual sausages in haste, with the resultant digestive upsets.

It cannot be emphasized too strongly that the first seven years of life are the most important for the religious development of the child and that in these seven years he is not capable of religious experience in the sense in which the adult understands it. His experiences in this period prepare him for religion, and his later religious outlook depends on them. His religion is not a surface veneer and it will not be something injected into him at a later time, after the years of infancy, as a kind of optional extra, but will grow out of what he has experienced in those years. Awareness of this fact should guide us into the right methods of religious education.

In the first two years the problem of what direct religious instruction to give the child does not arise, since the child is incapable of understanding any instruction. His mind is not sufficiently developed. Some parents believe, however, that they should accustom their child to a religious atmosphere from the very beginning by praying over him each night, or at any rate saying their prayers in the presence of the child, thus surrounding him with an atmosphere of devotion. They hope that the child will absorb this atmosphere and that devotion will then become a natural attitude in him.

Now, it is true that young children are extremely sensitive to the emotional atmosphere around them, almost as if they had telepathic awareness of what is in the minds of their parents. Parents should take note of this. It is impossible to disguise from young children the emotional states of the mother in particular. If there is conflict between the parents, the child soon becomes aware of it, however much the parents may try to hide it. In the same way he is responsive to the states of fear, anxiety, depression, worry, on the one hand, or to joyousness and serenity on the other.

We do not really need to postulate telepathic awareness to explain this. We betray our emotional states by a multitude of bodily changes of which we are rarely conscious. Indeed, one theory of the emotions – the one most strongly held – is that the characteristic feelings that mark them consist simply of the perception of the complex of muscular and visceral changes that take place when we are confronted with a situation that calls forth that particular reaction. The young child perceives these changes and so becomes aware of what the parent is feeling. Sometimes, by a kind of sympathy, he goes on to experience a similar emotion in himself. If the mother is anxious, her baby is likely to suffer from anxiety as well.

The parents, therefore, should hesitate about praying over the baby with the intention of training him in religion. I say nothing about the questionableness of using prayers to God as a means of influencing someone else. I am not speaking of intercessory prayers made on behalf of the baby, but of prayers that are made into a psychological tool to influence the development of the baby. If the parents try to use their prayers in this way, there is an element of insincerity in them, for instead of being addressed in spirit to God they are directed at the baby. The danger is that the baby will detect this insincerity and the prayers will have the opposite effect from that intended. In other words, we should not adopt this practice of praying over the baby as a means of religious education. It has value only when it comes naturally and spontaneously to the parents and they do not see it as having any effect upon the baby at all. They are simply trying to bring the baby into their act of thanksgiving and praise.

The most important thing is not whether the prayers are said in the presence of the baby, but whether the parents are worshipping people. If they are religious, the young child will sense their devotion and it will leave its imprint on him. It is not what they do to the child but what they are that counts for most. It is useless to put on a show of religion for the sake of the child, if they are not fundamentally religious. On the other hand, the fact that the parents are not professedly practising believers does not debar the child from becoming religious at a later stage.

The very anxiety of religious people to give their children a religious upbringing often leads them into errors from which the non-religious are free, namely, of imposing religion on the young child before he is able to receive it and creating in him an aversion to it. Children brought up in pious homes all too frequently revolt against religion as soon as they are able to speak for themselves.

But we should distinguish between excessive piety and true devoutness of life. It is doubtful whether excess of piety is a sign of true religion; it is one of the aberrations of religion, a pseudo-religion. If we make this distinction, we can then say that it is to the future advantage of the baby to have religious parents, because the impact of their attitudes on him will predispose him to grow into a religious person.

Far more significant for the future religious development of the child are those factors that have no appearance of religion at all, to which attention was drawn in the first part of this book, namely, the relations with his mother and the handling of his aggression. Something needs to be added to what was then said, for we were then considering the unfolding of the baby's mind. The mother has an active role to play in stimulating and fostering the development of the baby. In these first two years she is everything to him. (It would take us too far afield to enter into a discussion of those cases where a baby is deprived of his mother and is reared by a substitute mother. What is said of the natural mother holds for the foster mother, except, of course, that the latter finds it difficult, and in some respects – for example, breast-feeding the baby – impossible to play the full part of a mother.)

Let us take first the handling of the baby's aggression. This is part of the general relation between mother and baby, but it is one that enables us to see in a fairly simple form the importance of the mother–baby relationship. We saw that if the baby's aggressive instincts are aroused violently and repeatedly, the task of controlling his rage is too difficult for him, and in consequence he may have to resort to turning the aggression in upon itself, treating the primary rage as an enemy. The effect is that the baby is attacking himself. The consequences of this are serious.

In the first place a division is created in the self at an early age, which means that it will be profound and enduring. So far as subsequent religious development is concerned, the way is opened for a number of evil results, any or all of which may manifest themselves in one form or another in a given person. One of the most obvious is that the primary aggressive instincts are not assimilated to the rest of the personality, but are violently repressed into the unconscious, out of which they are continually trying to erupt in disguised form, or towards substitute objects.

Since the first object of aggression was the mother who had failed to deal with his needs, and the mother is the source of love and of all good things to the baby, the unresolved aggression is still aimed at love. Anyone in the grip of this dissociation or division of personality is therefore liable to be suspicious of love or of anyone who proffers good things, because in doing so they take the place of the mother. Such a person, therefore, cannot wholeheartedly accept God as love, or trust him. If he believes in God at all, it is likely to be in a God on to whom he projects his own repressed aggressive impulses, a cruel and vengeful God, who takes delight in punishing. He builds his God on the pattern of his own unconscious, and gets his pleasure from indulging his aggression through God, instead of directly. On the other hand, because he longs for love, for we cannot live without it, life is a continual frustration because his aggression prevents him from accepting love.

In *Civilization and Its Discontents* Sigmund Freud declares that Christianity, in asking for complete renunciation of aggression and its replacement by love, is asking more than is possible to human nature and that which, therefore, ought not to be asked. It is no answer to his criticism to cite against it that 'with God all things are possible', for that, in effect, denies the possibility of a full psychological study of human behaviour, since parts of it are put beyond the reach of description in scientific terms. These are held to be unconnected with the ordinary processes of mental activity, that is not explicable in terms of them.

To assume that changes take place in the mind that are not continuous with previous states of the mind is to give up all hope of explanation and to deny the validity of the great insights that have been won by workers in this field, such as the great pioneer, William James. Moreover, such an assumption can be challenged as contradicting the principle of incarnation, that God uses 'natural' means to convey his 'supernatural' revelation and to achieve his purposes. It is a central tenet of the Christian faith that he does so. In any case, even if the assumption were sound, it would still be necessary to examine the state of mind of the individual who had thus had his aggression resolved, in the effort to discover what had become of it.

Freud's criticism has to be faced honestly and not

evaded by resort to pious obscurantism. Aggression is a very strong natural endowment and, as is only too obvious, it is one of the most powerful forces at work in the world, both in public and in private life, in a multitude of forms. Christian educators tend to underestimate its power. We try to deal with it by diverting it into innocuous channels, such as sport and other forms of competition, and flatter ourselves that we are sublimating it. Or we try to turn it into a virtue by directing it to an attack upon disease, evil, and ignorance, and embody it in the Church in the form of the Church Militant. In their place, these may be useful and necessary, but whatever the form it takes and the object at which it is aimed, it is still the enemy of love.

I have recently seen a saying attributed to the great Russian writer, Chekhov, 'Love, friendship, respect do not unite people as much as a common hatred for something.' In time of war (hot or cold) we can be a united people because we have a common object of hate at which to direct our aggression. Without that safety valve we hate one another, openly or secretly, and the growth of love in us is choked. The appalling thing is that our very desire and need for love can thus drive us to hate, for by finding an object to hate we can love more freely, if in a limited area. In religion the devil serves a useful purpose, for by hating him we can love our neighbours and God with more zest!

It must be admitted that so far Christianity has failed to solve the problem of handling aggression, even among Christians. It does not necessarily follow that it cannot be solved. We have failed to understand the fullness of Christianity and have been content to think that the way to treat aggression is to restrain it. This is also Freud's assumption in the argument quoted. We even go further and think we can sometimes bless aggression in the name of the God of love.

My belief is that the Christian religion requires us to

absorb aggression – our own as well as that directed against us – and that this is demanded, not only by a true Christianity, but for the welfare of all men. I am therefore constrained to believe that aggression can be integrated into the personality so that it always functions in subordination to constructive aims and never for the pleasure of destructiveness that simple indulgence in it brings. There is a limited amount of evidence to support this view, though it cannot be said to be anything approaching proof. The chief weight behind my belief is the pre-eminence of love in life, for love is the source of all creativeness, and life means creativeness. Life is worthless and even impossible if aggression can ultimately defeat love. The goal of Christianity is to see 'Death swallowed up in victory' – death, which is the aim of aggression; victory, which is creative achievement. Perhaps this takes us too far afield, but what follows is based on the assumption that in the handling of children it is not only desirable but possible to reduce the amount of free aggression to a minimum.

We do not solve the problem of aggression by diverting it to objects far removed from its original aim, for while there is unassimilated aggression in us it is likely to catch us in another way. We have seen that the infant, in the effort to control his rages, which he treats as an enemy, turns some of it in upon himself and that this becomes associated with his conscience when this takes a moral form about the age of five. In that case his strength of conscience is not derived from his moral perceptions, and his judgements, especially his condemnatory ones, will always be distorted, because the need to punish and destroy will be a powerful element in them, even when it is cloaked under the guise of righteous indignation and horror of evil. The cruelties of religious persecutions, such as those of the Inquisition, are sufficient demonstration of how the lust to destroy can pervert even the desire to serve God.

Or it can be seen in the way many religious people relish the thought of hell-fire, for sinners, of course, not for themselves. They project their aggressive impulses on to God and thereby try to justify them.

Even if aggression does not break out in this way, it defeats our moral and religious development (and our general health of personality) in a way that is probably almost universal. It creates in us a sense of guilt. This sense of guilt may be conscious or unconscious or partly both. Our self-directed aggression creates in us the tension that we experience as guilt, as self-condemnation. The evidence from psychotherapy seems to indicate that at the core of every neurosis there is an unconscious guilt complex, the hardest to shift, standing in the way of a complete cure. To acknowledge its existence to ourselves is to admit an infantile hatred of our mother – the 'bad' mother – the meaning and source of life to us, so it would be a confession that we are afraid that life is not worth living. To make that acknowledgement, therefore, requires supreme courage, which few of us possess. We try to keep our sense of guilt instead, and so avoid giving up our aggressiveness.

We are not concerned here with the psychological issues involved but with the development of religion, so we need not explore that point further. In religion, emphasis is frequently laid on the need to feel a sense of guilt, and much preaching is directed to producing it. This is due to a confusion between the realization of sinfulness and the sense of guilt. Simple reflection would tell us that if a sense of guilt were the same as repentance and repentance is turning towards God or the good, we are indeed a godly people, for the sense of guilt is universal. The sense of guilt is futile; it achieves nothing, except the discomfort of inward conflict. Its essence is to keep the *status quo*. Or rather, it is like an accountant's balance sheet, in which one side has to equal the other. When we suffer from guilt, we are comparing what we have done, or desired to do, with the standards that we have set up. We judge by ourselves, by our ideal selves, and our judgement not only says how bad we have been but also, by implication, how good we are in our 'real', that is, ideal, selves. That is why people get so much satisfaction out of confessing how bad they have been, for it is the same as saying how good they are to hold the standards of conduct they do.

The sense of sin, or, to use a less misleading phrase, the recognition of our sinfulness, is something different. It is the honest objective perception of how far short we have fallen from what is good. The judgement follows from our perception of something good outside or beyond ourselves. We get a fresh vision of God, or the good, which enlarges our understanding of him, and in the light of that new understanding we know that we have 'missed the mark', as the Greek of the New Testament describes sin.

We know our ideals as well as our deeds to be inadequate, and the result of it is always a turning to God, not a furious turning upon ourselves. The true sense of sin directs us to God, whereas the sense of guilt focuses our attention upon ourselves by saying that we have not been true to ourselves. The 'guilty' person thinks he could have done better. The repentant knows that he could not have done so and openly admits it. He does not then lash himself with self-reproaches as the guilt-laden man does, but seeks from God the strength and the wisdom to do better.

If we seem to have wandered far from our theme, it is not so. It should be clear from what has been said that this type of conscience, which is obsessed with guilt, is an obstacle to true religious development. Since the sense of guilt comes very largely from the overdevelopment of aggression in the very early years of childhood, one of the essential foundations for later religious life lies in the right handling of the aggressive instincts of the child. This must first be done by the mother. It is done in the context of her ordinary maternal relations with him – feeding him, nursing him, bathing him, playing with him – and not in any specific religious setting.

Some of the ways in which the aggressive instincts of the baby are most likely to arise have been indicated in Chapter 8 and suggestions for dealing with them were also given there. The general aim of the mother should be to minimize the outbursts of aggression as much as possible by taking thought in advance of how to avoid the frustrations that may occasion it and by learning to recognize it in the young baby and dealing with it promptly. In the first few months this will be largely negative action, that is, preventing the aggression that is part of the natural equipment of the child from getting loose. He is too young to be able to handle it effectively. As he grows and develops interests in play, he gains more strength to deal with it, but he will still need the help of his mother in the ways indicated.

In this way parents are most surely preparing the way for the future religious health of the child. Before he can come to terms with God, he has to come to terms with the world. He must learn confidence to deal with the experiences that come to him, and one of the hardest tasks with which he can be faced is that of assimilating aggressiveness. In this as elsewhere, prevention is better, and easier, than cure, hence the importance of the care the mother must take in understanding and meeting the needs of her baby as they arise.

CHAPTER 11

THE EARLY YEARS: THE ROOTS OF LOVE

THE great contribution the mother makes to the religious development of the child is to show him what love means, by the way she treats him and by setting free his own power to love, in the secure setting of her love that she has created around him. To succeed in this she has to fulfil two primary tasks. They are, first, to help him handle his aggression satisfactorily, and, second, to build up the right kind of interpersonal relations with him, in which neither unduly dominates the other but there is a free give-and-take between them. The first is negative, to protect the child from having to face too great a trial for the strength he has at the particular period of his growth. We have looked at that in the previous chapter. The second is positive: to draw him on into growth, developing and setting free his love. The more successfully this is achieved, the less difficulty there is in handling his aggression.

In this connexion it is important to remind ourselves again that religion is not something grafted superficially on to the personality; religion is what the whole person becomes by its growth, and therefore, at this stage, as indeed at all stages, the mother's aim must be to foster the full unfolding of the potential personality of her baby.

The key word is 'interpersonal'. We are talking about a relationship between two persons, with the mutual adaptation, responses, and interpenetration that is always involved in personal relationships. The mother–baby relationship, however, is a peculiar one, because the mother is an adult conscious of her self-identity, her personality long since formed and stable, and inevitably seeing her baby as hers, even as part of herself, whereas the baby's personality is only beginning to take shape, and he is as yet unconscious of self-identity, living from moment to moment, unable to look ahead and plan for the future. The mother must take the lead. She must do the planning for the baby's future, both near and distant. She must plan for the next stage of his growth, and she must have in mind the end of that growth when he shall have become a full-grown person.

An essential part of the relationship is the mother's discovery of the character of her baby. Each child has his own particular endowment, and even within the same family there is a wide range of differences among children. The strength of their instinctive impulses, their temperaments, their native intelligence, all vary and affect their development considerably. They grow in different aspects and at different rates, both bodily and mentally. Each child is an individual, and what helps one may not help another; and even with the same child his development dictates the kind of help he requires at any time from his mother. This means that no hard-and-fast system of rules can be laid down for bringing up children. All that can be given are the general principles that should govern the relationship between the mother and her baby, and she must adapt them to the particular child. This is true, of course, not only in the mother phase, the first two years, but in the later years of infancy as well.

The first of these principles is that the mother must try to discover the nature of her baby. He is so small, so helpless, so dependent on her, that she will be tempted to treat him as a plaything, a precious possession, a little bit of herself that she wants to keep like that forever. She ought to look ahead and envisage the time when he has to be independent of her, and seeing that, treat him as a person from the beginning, work for his growth. She must begin the process of weaning him from herself, and herself from him, by seeing him at once as an individual over against herself.

The second principle is closely related to this. The mother must not try to impose upon her baby her own ideal pattern of what she wants him to be, or thinks he ought to be, a pattern arrived at without taking into account his individual abilities and character. To attempt this may impose demands upon him that he cannot meet. Rather must she aim at developing what is in the child, by promoting growth from within and, subject to the need to fit into the family, allowing it to take its own shape. She should steer the growth, not try to compel it to take preconceived forms. If she has taken pains to understand his character, this will be easier than might be thought at first sight.

Parents do not as a rule realize the extent to which they try to make their children fit into a preformed pattern. Various things dictate it. They want their child to be as neat and quiet as Mrs Jones's baby next door. They want him to learn self-control even earlier than the Jones's baby. They want him to be like other babies, or the kind of baby they have read about in their manual of child care. They want him to be intelligent and beautiful (if a girl), handsome (if a boy), and successful.

Many children have their lives made miserable because their parents are dominated by conventional ideas of what a child ought to be, and what interests he ought to have. Almost always, too, the parents are moved by unconscious motives. In their own childhood they felt themselves to be misunderstood and deprived or thwarted – or they look back to their childhood and imagine this happened – and they try, without realizing they are doing so, to relive their childhood in their own children and get from them the emotional satisfactions they feel they missed, and they seek to fulfil their disappointed ambitions in them. In consequence they try to take possession of the life of the child and live again in him, not allowing him his own free life. One of the hardest tasks confronting parents is to let their children be themselves.

This does not mean that there should be no restrictions and inhibitions placed on the child or that he is not to be subjected to discipline. He needs help to control his own impulses, and the right kind of discipline will help him in this. This is clear from the third principle of treatment, that the child has to be helped to take his place in the social group, the family, and that the family has its rights, whether it be the parents or other children. All must accommodate themselves in their demands on the baby to what he is capable of giving. He is not strong enough yet to bear much frustration and deprivation. In the first two years he has no understanding of his place in the family and therefore cannot be held to have responsibilities towards it. His mother, however, has responsibilities to the rest of the family, and these cannot be totally put aside for the sake of the newcomer. She must share her love and attentions among all the children, otherwise she is doing hurt to the older ones and by doing so creating a bad family atmosphere for the baby.

One of the causes of resentment in older children is the trauma they suffer when a new baby seems to take away their mother's love and attention from them. She must from the beginning try to incorporate the baby into the family group. Jealousy of the newcomer is bound to manifest itself in older children, especially in the next oldest. This is natural and should not be treated as a sign of 'naughtiness' or bad disposition. It will be minimized if the mother shows by her behaviour that the advent of the baby does not in the least reduce the mother's love for the older children. If she has to give more time and attention to the baby it is because of his helplessness, whereas she can praise the older ones for their ability to fend for themselves. So far as is practicable she can get their help in looking after the baby, fetching clothes, preparing the bath, and so on. It is a great help to give the younger ones some special gift at the birth of the baby, such as a doll for the girls, or a pet, so that they have a 'baby' of their own and can identify themselves with the mother and develop the same kind of feelings of care and responsibility that she feels to the newcomer. In these ways she is trying to foster positive attitudes in them towards the baby.

Above everything else, the mother should enjoy her association with the baby. Here is what one of the greatest child experts in Britain says to mothers of newly born babies:

> Enjoy being thought important. Enjoy letting other people look after the world while you are producing a new one of its members. Enjoy being turned-in and almost in love with yourself, the baby is so nearly a part of you. Enjoy the way in which your man feels responsible for the welfare of you and your baby. Enjoy finding out new things about yourself. Enjoy having more right than you have ever had before to do just what you feel is good. Enjoy being annoyed with the baby when cries and yells prevent acceptance of the milk that you long to be generous with. Enjoy all sorts of womanly feelings that you cannot even start to explain to a man. Particularly, I know you will enjoy the signs that gradually appear that the baby is a person, and that you are recognized as a person by the baby.
>
> Enjoy all this for your own sake, but the pleasure which you can get out of the messy business of infant care happens to be vitally important from the baby's point of view. The baby does not want to be given the correct feed at the correct time, so much as to be fed by someone who loves feeding her own baby. The baby takes for granted all things like the softness of the clothes and having the bath water at the right temperature. What cannot be taken for granted is the mother's pleasure that goes with the clothing and bathing of her own

baby. The mother's pleasure has to be there or else the whole procedure is dead, useless, and mechanical.*

This book is of outstanding importance, both for the understanding of the child and for hints on treating him.

There are many very helpful books on child care, but there are also many that are not so helpful, because they overlook the primary importance of this factor of personal love. They overrate the relative importance of hygiene, systematic feeding, proceeding according to rule – the bodily factors. These are important, of course, but the most delicate part of a baby is his mental and emotional life, the core of his personality. It is this side of him that needs the most care. Rules are only a rough guide to help the mother, and she should be ready to break them if the needs of her baby seem to make it advisable. Nothing can take the place of the love she shows him by her delight in him.

Mothers are naturally anxious to bring up their children in the best way possible, and because they feel the great responsibility that lies upon them they grow anxious about it, afraid lest they make a mistake. They run to this or that handbook for guidance, and any that speak with an air of authority and give clear-cut systems that can be followed easily make a special appeal. The young mother, in particular, feels so helpless and inexperienced before the frailty and dependence of her baby. Perhaps what has been written in these pages has contributed to the anxiety of some, because the importance of the mother has been so heavily emphasized. If that is the case, I can only hasten to assure the mother not to worry, for nature has armed you with the one thing that you need to carry the responsibility – your love for your baby. Your love for him, your play with him, your admiration of him, and your patience

* D. W. Winnicott, *The Child, the Family, and the Outside World*, Pelican Books, 1964, pp. 26–7.

with him are far more valuable than any system that has been devised. Order and system belong to a later stage. While he is a baby, follow Dr Winnicott's advice: relax and enjoy your baby.

Just as nature has provided the mother with the love the baby needs, so it has equipped the baby with a tremendous power of response to it. Her love releases in him a love in return, which helps him to grow. Because he finds the world so satisfying and so welcoming, he reaches out towards it with zest and confidence. He is better able to bear temporary pains and frustrations because he has been strengthened by the warmth of her love. Those needs: hunger, cold, and so on, began as disturbances to his peace and therefore as enemies, but his mother enabled them to turn into delights by her delight and fellowship with him as she deals with them.

Of course, the baby cannot think in these terms, but *he goes through the experience* described by them, and they no doubt remain as a series of images in his mind. By not depriving him too long, the mother is thus helping him to bear deprivation when it comes. Later on, of course, she will have to help him bear longer periods of deprivation, but that will be when he has learned to look ahead and wait. He has to learn a sense of time, and he cannot learn it quickly. In learning to love, he is learning to trust. Fear of having lost or destroyed the loved object will be less powerful in him, and consequently he will be less aggressive also. His aggression will be drawn into his zest for living and will strengthen his love.

In the Christian sacrament of Holy Communion, the core of Christian worship, Christ feeds the worshipper upon his spiritual body and blood, just as the mother fed her baby from her own body. There is much more in the sacrament than this, but there is an essential connexion, for as the love of the mother was made known to her baby in the act of feeding in the first place, so the love of God is made real to the baby after he has grown up in the spiritual feeding that he offers, whereby (to quote the Anglican liturgy) 'He dwells in us and we in him'.

By their mutual love and delight in each other, the mother dwells in the baby and the baby in the mother. His experience of this deep personal relationship with his mother remains in his mind and prepares the way for his later understanding of the way God imparts himself to men. It has to be developed and enriched by other experiences, notably by his personal encounter with his father, but it is the essential first step in the child's religious education. Whoever has not experienced this rich human relationship at the beginning of his life will be gravely handicapped in appreciating what religion has to offer, as well as in other aspects of his life. The mother is mediating the love of God to her baby by a kind of natural sacrament.

The mother need not be afraid of spoiling her child by giving him too much love in the first two years. He needs as much love as he can get, provided it is constant and spontaneous. Spoiling is the outcome of uncertainty in the baby's mind. It can be the result of contradictory attitudes on the part of the mother. If she is neglectful at one moment and overdemonstrative at the next, she creates an uncertainty in his mind. The extremes are too wide apart for him to assimilate them. He then becomes afraid of losing the 'good' mother and becomes terrified of the 'bad' mother, who makes him suffer, and of his aggressive impulses towards her. He therefore clings all the more desperately to his 'good' mother and is afraid to let her out of his sight.

He is also afraid to face the world, afraid to grow up and accept novelty with equanimity, because his security has been undermined by the tensions to which he has already been subjected. He is always demanding assurances and proofs of love. The mother's love should therefore be steady and continuous, not something that has to be earned by obedience and good conduct, but is, on the contrary, completely dependable. Of course, circumstances beyond the control of the mother may have an adverse effect on the child. He may, for instance, contract some illness or meet with some accident that causes him to suffer and perhaps even separates him from his mother for a while. This can happen, too, if the mother herself falls ill. The child cannot be protected from every possibility of harm of this kind. Nor should the mother be over-anxious about protection for him. He has to learn to accept some degree of hardship and suffering. If the mother is over-anxious, she infects her baby with anxiety for which he knows no reason, and this takes away his sense of security and confidence in his mother. She simply needs to go on cheerfully loving him all the time, anticipating his needs, comforting his hurts, and displaying her lively interest in him.

If, for any reason, there is a breakdown in the good relationship between the mother and her baby, one consequence may be of considerable importance in his religious development. The baby has the sense of having lost the mother. This creates a wound in his mind so deep that he will all his life be seeking to recover her and the love and attention that go with her. He may do this in many ways that have nothing direct to do with religion at all. Frequently, however, he turns to religion and finds in the Church the ideal mother whom he had lost. He will give her all the devotion that he longed to give to his mother as a baby. In return he will seek security and protection from her. She is the safeguard he needs against the loneliness that loss of his mother fixed in him; she is his security against all adversities; she it is who finally restores him to happiness by ensuring his place in heaven where he is freed from all hardship and suffering. This is a common religious type, and there is something of it in all of us. It is, however, open to question whether it is really religious at all, because it is fundamentally based on fear of the world and a shrinking from hardship and suffering. A mature religion cannot be derived from fear of the world. A mature religion remembers the sayings, 'Be strong, and of a good courage', and 'I have overcome the world'.

One more thing needs to be said before we leave this period of development, though it applies to the whole time of growing up of the child. The baby is growing, and his needs change from day to day. Because the mother enjoys his babyhood so much, when he is utterly dependent upon her, she is constantly tempted to ignore his growing and to try to treat him as a baby forever. This holds back his development and creates serious tension in him.

The law of growth is irresistible and pushes him forward. The mother who tries to hold him back is doing it for her own pleasure, even when she says, and thinks, that she is doing it for his good, protecting him from risk or from effort. If she is to play the part of a good mother, she must turn him gradually away from herself towards the world. The process of weaning, we said above, begins at birth. The treatment needed by a new-born baby does not suit the one-year-old. The mother must always be looking ahead, encouraging the independence of her child. It is only when he is fully self-reliant and independent of her that she can be sure of a permanent love between them. When her task is completed and her baby has grown into a mature personality, a full personal bond is possible between them. Possessive love destroys that bond.

This is illustrated by the following account given of himself by Anatole France:

Look you, my friend, there is something worse than hate, worse than indifference: it is love, tyrannous love. . . . I had myself the most loving of mothers. She worshipped her only son, her Anatole, as her masterpiece, her darling. . . . I received double my portion of love. It was much, my friend; far too much. She literally poisoned my life. She made me foolish and stupid, vacillating and timid. Accustomed, because of her, to leading-strings right up to my thirtieth year, I shrank from crossing that abyss in life which separates adolescence from manhood! We were both of us ridiculous. Did she speak of me – me, a bearded man – she represented me as a little child.

Until I was thirty-five my mother never went to bed until I had returned home. At midnight, or even at four o'clock in the morning, I would find her silent and relentless, candle in hand. It became a sort of religious ceremony. . . .

Up to the time of my marriage my mother always tucked me up in bed. When she kissed me I sometimes had the desire to strangle her. There is no tyranny more heavy than that of maternal love.*

It was Bernard Shaw, I think, who said, 'If there is anyone a well-brought-up English girl hates more than her eldest sister, it is her mother!'

His mother's love is the greatest need of a young child but, because it is so important to him, it is equally dangerous when it goes wrong. Her love is therefore at its best when it is a free gift to him, not a greedy demand to hold him to her. It must partake of the character of God's love, which desires only the welfare of the beloved. Demanding love, greedy love, which seeks to take full possession of the object of love, is not love at all, for it destroys love by choking off the capacity to love in that which it seeks to enslave.

By her love, it was said above, the mother is mediating the love of God to her child in a natural sacrament; but if she is to give him the right kind of love, creative and not possessive love, she needs to be aware of this connexion between her love and God's love; she needs to be living in a conscious relationship with God. Not by teaching her baby religion, but being God-filled herself, will she open the way to God for him.

* Quoted by G. F. Morton, *Childhood's Fears*, Duckworth & Co., 1925, p. 61, from *Anatole France en Pantoufles*.

CHAPTER 12

LATER INFANCY: QUESTIONS ABOUT GOD

THE later years of infancy, from three to seven years of age, are the most difficult period in the religious development of the child, particularly for the parents. The young child of this age is still incapable of understanding religious ideas and motives, but to unwary parents or teachers he may seem to be understanding them while all the time he has misunderstood them, given them his own interpretation. He may say his 'prayers', talk about God, sing the hymns he is taught, and so on, giving the outward appearance of being religious, but to the child himself what he does has another significance altogether. It may be just an interesting game, playing at being grown up, or just something to please Father or Mother or the teacher, or, more likely, the satisfaction of fantasies that are going on in the child's mind about his relations with his parents and other people in his environment. If pressure is brought upon him, either by the accidents of circumstance or by a deliberate effort on the part of his parents, to try to make him religious in the adult sense of the term, he is likely to become fixed in his infantile misunderstanding. The ideas and feelings he has about these new activities will be overdeveloped by the emphasis put upon them, making it difficult for him to pass smoothly out of them on the way to truer understanding of what religion is.

This does not mean that he ought to be sheltered entirely from such teaching. In most cases that is impossible. Religious activity of various kinds is part of his daily environment, even when his family is not active in religion. He cannot be insulated from it, even if that were desirable. He will become curious about the things that he sees and will ask questions about it, questions that ought to be answered. What is most important is not to mistake the religious behaviour of the child as true religion.

The attempt to shield him from religion is just as likely to have a bad effect and handicap his later approach to it. A typical illustration of this was given to me by an agnostic friend. Neither he nor his wife makes any practice of religion and they give no teaching to their little girls, aged seven and five. Recently they were driving through Oxford, the little girls sitting in the back of the car and keeping up a running commentary on what they saw. Presently they passed a church. The older of the two dropped her voice to a hushed whisper, as though to protect her parents from something that would be painful to them, and explained to her sister, 'That is a church!' My friend did not know how she had got the knowledge, but obviously she had already invested it with false emotional significance that would make it hard for her to approach it later with the matter-of-factness that is necessary to a healthy appraisal of religion.

The problem of parents is that of finding the middle way. The parents of the girls just referred to had made no active attempt to bring religion before them, but had simply ignored it because it played little or no part in their own lives. At the other extreme we have those who try to train their children from the beginning in religious beliefs and practices with great earnestness and piety. The consequences may be even more disastrous for the children.

The parents do not and cannot pass on to their children the ideas and ideals they are trying to impart, for the latter have not acquired sufficient experience to grasp them. Instead, they interpret the teaching in the light of the mental equipment they have built up in the limited circumstances of their short term of life. And to their interpretation they attach the emotional values they have caught from their parents. One of the most firmly established truths about the working of the mind is that it can receive only that which previous experience, and reflection over experience, has prepared it to assimilate. If something novel is thrust upon it, the mind can absorb only the portion of it that corresponds to something previously encountered, or twists the new experience to fit the pattern of a familiar one already held.

A simple illustration will make this clear. A man's somewhat unusual behaviour may be inexplicable and even frightening to one observer, who can only try to account for it in empty general terms such as mental collapse; to a second observer it is a relatively simple case of hysteria, symptomatic of certain strains and stresses within the man's personality; a third observer is convinced that the man is possessed by a demon. Each interprets, or fails to interpret, according to the knowledge and experience he has amassed.

Behind the parents' religion lie many years of experience, giving it its shape and meaning far beyond the capacity of the child. This means that religious language and acts have a vastly different significance for them from what they have for the child. The words they use, because they are so familiar, seem to have a simple, straightforward meaning. They do not realize how much this depends on familiarity. They are alerted if they see that the child does not understand. The danger is when the child appears to understand but in actual fact misunderstands, that is, understands in his own way with meanings different from those intended by the parents. Conversely, the parents may read into the child's sayings and doings meanings that are derived from their experience, not the child's.

When we come to examine what religion can mean to a young child, we have to consider carefully what mental equipment he has to enable him to deal with it, what the ideas and images are that he has formed. We have discussed this in some detail, and here we need only to remind ourselves of the general conclusion.

We saw first that his mind has been formed by his experiences in the family circle, and that in this second half of infancy he is wrestling with conflicting ideas and impulses that turn around his relations with his mother and father. In consequence of the diverse and contradictory pulls that his instincts and his experience with his parents make upon him, he forms images of a good mother and a bad mother, of a good father and a bad father, as though he had different sets of parents. The reason for this is, we saw, that the images are not the result of the objective perception of his parents, but correspond to the emotional stresses he feels and the satisfactions that he gets from his parents. The degree of goodness and badness is determined by the strength of his emotions, rather than corresponding to the character of his parents. Of course, their behaviour may be of such kind as to rouse strong emotions in him and intensify his fantasy images.

This is the period of great imaginativeness. The young child's mind is extremely active, possibly more so than at any other epoch of his life; but, lacking a full command of words, he does his thinking by means of images and the laws of their association. It is difficult for an adult, particularly an educated adult – such as one capable of understanding this book – to recapture the dominance of images and the strong overtones of feeling that go with them. Adults have been trained to the constant use of words and abstract logical processes of thinking. These have replaced thinking by images. But the young child has only images as his mental tools, and extends his knowledge by extending the application of the images he has formed. Further, he is not able to draw clear distinctions between image and reality, between what goes on in the world outside himself and what is in his mind. It is not long since he came to the realization of himself as a person separate from his mother. It takes a long time and much experience to enable us to learn the boundaries of our subjective experience. Most of us never succeed in doing it completely in every respect, but retain areas where our feelings, our preconceptions, determine our perceptions and our judgements. If the young child holds ideas about his parents that seem extravagant to an adult, that is because he is a child and thinks and feels as a child.

We can apply this to the child's understanding of God. At some stage he will ask who or what God is. To find the right answer to this – right in the sense of helping on the child's development – is a major problem for parents. Consider some of the probable answers: 'God made the world'; 'God is our Father in heaven'; 'God sent Jesus into the world' (presuming that the child has been told stories about Jesus); 'God is everywhere, able to do anything, knows everything'. These answers may be further elaborated in a doctrinal way to impress on the child the idea that God requires us to be good and that he is offended and will punish us if we do wrong. This kind of teaching may be given in answer to questions, or it may be deliberately taught to the child at home or in Sunday school.

What can he get out of it? There can be no question of his grasping the theological or philosophical meaning of the idea. It is far too abstract a conception to be within his powers. Adults find it very difficult to say concisely what they mean by God, for definitions like 'ultimate reality', 'supreme being', 'the ground of existence', 'the Absolute', have a precise meaning only for those highly trained in philosophy.

Infinite means to most people something very, very large, rather than something differing in quality, not quantity, from the finite. Most of us have to admit that when we think about God in intimate terms, we usually have in our minds some picture, or series of pictures, perhaps vivid, perhaps so vague that we do not realize it is a picture unless we are led to analyse it carefully. A theologian friend of mine, who has one of the most brilliant and penetrating minds I have ever known, confessed to me that when he says his prayers there is apt to flash into his mind the image of a picture that used to hang in his nursery when he was a small boy, depicting some angels in the sky with the figure or face of a benign old man in the background of the sky – God.

We can think about God only by means of some such representation of him – not necessarily so crude or naïve as that one. Almost always we think of him as an exalted man, and try to escape from our anthropomorphism by extending human capacities to infinity, describing God as omnipotent, omniscient, omnipresent, of infinite love and mercy. I do not mean to imply that there is no value in thinking this way, or that we can escape from it. All I ask is that we recognize that we are thinking in metaphors and analogies, largely of a pictorial nature. The child thinks in the same way, but he has not the range of experience to formulate some of the metaphors that adults use and take for granted.

The young child has, however, an image ready to hand by which to interpret the idea of God when he comes upon it. It is that which he has formed of his father in the years three to five, or rather the images, for we saw that he sees his father under different aspects. Under both good and bad aspects the father appears to the young child as all-knowing and all-powerful. As good father, he is to be loved and admired; as bad father, to be feared and obeyed. The child is certain to apply one or both of these images to God. He seems to fit them exactly. Which image it will be depends on too many things to make it easy to control or forecast.

The attitude of the parents themselves must exercise a profound influence in this. If to them God is an exacting taskmaster, sitting in judgement forever, demanding unquestioning obedience to his law, they are likely to present God to the child as the bad father. By stressing the love and kindness of God, they may succeed in bringing him under the good father image. Probably in most cases God will appear under both.

If God appears as wholly good, and there is fixation in the infantile attitude, the bad father image has to be located somewhere. A common resort is to postulate Satan as the author of all evil and the prompter to sin. If God appears wholly under the bad father image, and again in case of fixation, he has to be rejected later and a good father image found in his stead – some secular leader or hero. If God appears under both, the child is left with contradictory ideas about him and in case of fixation will find it impossible to reconcile them. God will then be neither wholly moral nor wholly loving and will create despair in those who see him thus.

The danger is of fixation in this infantile attitude. It does not require a very profound knowledge of religious beliefs to recognize how widespread these infantile views of God are. The diverse pictures of God are to be found in all religions that proclaim him. He is loving Father and at the same time stern Judge. The infantile attitudes persist, because fixation in them is almost universal, to some degree at least.

There are three causes for this fixation. The first is that in these years the child is going through a very profound emotional development. It is a period of emotional disturbance and conflict in which each experience is felt with great intensity because the child has not yet achieved that inner coordination of the emotions that spreads the emotional pressure over the whole system instead of concentrating it into narrow channels. The ideas of the good and bad father are formed in the period of crisis, when the feelings are stretched almost to breaking point (it is the period of nightmares and fears – another manifestation of the emotionalism that marks it), and the idea of God is likely to take over this unbalanced emotion.

Second, the child cannot deal with God as he can with his father. The latter is there to be seen, listened to, touched. He can be compared with the images the child formed of him. They can be tested out by the reality and adjusted bit by bit. Bit by bit, too, the emotional pressure is lowered. This is a slow and laborious process, but it is part of growing up.

With God, however, it cannot be done. God is so far away in heaven, or so diffused through everything, that he cannot be seen or heard or touched. We can only hear about him. He cannot be got at. So there is no way open, at least no easy way, for the child to reduce the emotional pressure about God, or to adjust the infantile father ideas that were attached to him. These ideas of the father did not correspond to the real father, but were shaped by the child's emotional needs.

An untrue picture of the father is not likely to be a good foundation for a true picture of God. My theologian friend learned how to think correctly about God with one part of his mind, but another part was in sheer bondage to an infantile image from which he found it hard to escape. The infantile father-image God is a handicap to a clear appraisal of the positive indications we can later discover about the character and person of God.

The third factor making for fixation in infantile pictures of God is that the parents themselves, or teachers, find it hard to speak about God in a matter-of-fact voice, without some tinge of solemnity, sometimes of embarrassment. This may even be deliberate to impress the sacredness of God upon him. The child is immediately aware that there is something out of the ordinary involved, and it makes him uneasy, even afraid. God is somehow an awkward subject, something to be approached with caution.

As a result the child will be less ready to test out his ideas about God, the only way in which they can develop healthily.

To these may be added a fourth factor that sometimes is found. It acts as a shock to the child of this age to find the parents apparently acknowledging someone to be greater than they. To understand what this shock means, we have to recollect that the young child's experience is limited to his family, that apart from his father and mother everyone else is rather a vague or partial figure. As a secure foundation for subsequent development he needs the period in which he sees them as the perfection of love, goodness, beauty, and power. If God is greater than they are, he must be a bad person, because he takes away some of the perfection of the parents, an enemy to be feared and fought.

For these and other reasons, the topic of God is fraught with risk for the young child's future development in his religious ideas and attitudes, and the parents should realize how important it is to deal with it wisely. One thing clearly follows: no doctrinal or moralistic teaching should be forced upon the child. If he does not raise the topic of God, it should not be raised with him. Any religious teaching given in this period should be given only in answer to questions.

We are now in a better position to consider what is the right answer to give when children ask about God. There is no one right answer, for circumstances vary too much and each child is unique. The answer, however, must fulfil certain conditions.

In the first place, it must be an answer to the real question the child is asking. Children very easily mistake the meaning of words and phrases, or take literally what has only a metaphorical or idiomatic sense, like 'heaping coals of fire on an enemy's head' (by which I once startled a young child!) or 'take up your cross'.

There is a further obscurity in children's questions. On matters that have deep emotional significance for them, they are apt to ask the question following, instead of the direct one. That is to say, they observe or hear something, ponder over it, draw some conclusion from it, and ask the question about the latter. What they really want to know is whether their observation was correct. The question they ask is to test this. But it is also frequently a test of the parents too, a test to see how important they regard the topic that aroused interest in the first place. In answering a question, the parents need to take care that they understand the train of thought leading to the question; otherwise the answer they give may have very misleading consequences, for the child applies the answer, not to the question asked, but to the previous problem. For instance, a child may be prompted to ask about God because *some time before*, days past perhaps, he has heard his mother say that a baby brother or sister, towards whom he is feeling jealous, was 'sent by God'. In that case God is the cause of his trouble, and a careless answer that takes the question as an impersonal philosophic or scientific one could easily do damage to him.

Second, the answer should not go beyond what the child asks. Admittedly this is not always easy, but it is better to err on the side of brevity, because the child will ask further questions if he is not satisfied, whereas too long an answer frightens him. He got an unexpected reaction from his parent. So the question must have been a wrong one or a dangerous one.

Third, it should be an honest answer. If the parent is unable to answer it, he should admit it frankly. It will be a little shock to the child that there is something his father or mother does not know, but he has to discover this as he grows, and the shock is not so great as to discover his parents deceiving him. They cannot hide their own emotions from him, and he is rapidly aware of it when they try to tell him something for his good that they themselves do not believe.

Finally, the answer should show interest in the question, as an honest question deserving an honest and direct answer. The parents should be pleased at this sign of thoughtfulness in their child and show it by taking the question seriously and answering it to the best of their ability, not using it as the occasion to give an edifying discourse. As far as they can, they should try to answer it in terms that the child can understand, and in a matter-of-fact way. The important thing is that the child asks the question, and that is what is being dealt with. God may be very important to the parent, but he is not to the child, and cannot be, so the answer should not try to impose the parent's attitude on the child.

If these conditions are fulfilled it is relatively easy to give a helpful answer to the child's question. It is no use pretending that a full explanation of what God is can be given, and it will be necessary to make use of 'as if' and 'like'. 'God is like a father of everybody.' 'We talk to God as if he were with us, even when we cannot see him.' Or the answer can point to experience rather than comprehension – 'God is the name grown-ups give to all that is good in the world.'

The advantage of an answer like this is that it indicates by the use of 'grown-ups' that there is more to be discovered, and at the same time it prompts the child to go on thinking, because he has experience of good things. Moreover, he greatly desires to be grown up. The young child prefers to take one point at a time, absorb it, and come back later with supplementary questions. If he finds that his questioning is taken seriously and with respect, it helps him to overcome the fears that too readily attach to the image he has formed of God, and he is encouraged to go on seeking an objective approach to God instead of the subjective one that marks the period of infancy.

CHAPTER 13

CHURCHGOING AND PRAYER

RELIGIOUS activities form an integral part of the life of the community and, probably, of the child's family. Restricted though his life may be, the young child cannot avoid making some contact with these activities and having his interest aroused. We saw an instance of this in Chapter 12. He will ask many questions about what churches are for, and what goes on inside them and why. The same principles hold in answering these as for answers to those about God. To questions about churchgoing and public worship it is easier to give an answer that will satisfy the child, for it can be explained as something that grown-ups like doing. It may not prove necessary to go into theological explanations. Adults do many mysterious things that little children cannot understand, and churchgoing can be put among them. This does not mean, however, that the questions should be evaded. They need to be answered as simply and as factually as possible, without any elaborate justification for the actions in question, or any effort to impress and edify the child.

Prayer, however, is a risky topic. To explain to a young child what we are doing when we are praying is far from easy, and some of the answers bring in God and thereby raise the hazards we have already described. In explaining what prayer is, stress should not be laid on God's power to answer prayer. This is a difficult topic in any case, but it is made more difficult for the young child because he has not yet acquired the ability to draw a clear distinction between reality and fantasy.

In his fantasies he can make anything come true simply

by imagining it. Parents will get constant evidence of this power of fantasy in their children, normally in their play, but sometimes spreading into other activities as well. If God has the power to make anything 'come true', he is not governed by the principle of reality that the child is gradually learning to apply in the real world. Prayer will then come to be classified in the realm of fantasy, a way of escape from the limitations that hard matter of fact imposes upon us. It will be a kind of magic by which one can manipulate the world without making any effort. All one needs is the right formula, like 'open sesame', and the right approach to God the master magician. It may well happen later in his life that, seeing an opposition between science and religion, he will choose science as the way of reality, and reject religion because it means fantasy and magic to him.

The wiser answer, and one more within the comprehension of the child, is to explain praying in terms of our human activity. We tell the child that when we are praying we are trying to remember all the things that make us happy and saying a kind of 'thank you' for them, just because we are happy. When we pray for things to happen, we are trying to think of all the good or nice things that we should like to come true, and whether we really want them, but we ask for them in that way not just because we want them for ourselves but because we are trying to remember what will be nice for other people as well, and that it is easy for us to forget. And if people say their prayers together in church, that helps them to think of one another. The child can understand this because he has some experience of it himself and it focuses his attention on the effort of prayer rather than on the fantasy of easy achievement. He will have learned from his experience in wanting things that he is not allowed by his parents to get everything he wishes for.

Since children cannot understand what prayer and worship mean to an adult worshipper, they cannot be expected to pray like an adult. The question then arises as to whether they should be taught any form of prayer and worship at all. That is to say, should they be taken to church or Sunday school, learn to sing hymns and recite prayers, when we know that they are putting their own interpretation on them? Further, should they be taught at home to say their prayers, before going to bed, for instance?

There is no simple answer to these questions, because it depends very largely on the habits of the parents and what is going on around the child. One thing at least is clear, that if the parents are not themselves praying people, they are laying up trouble if they try to teach the children to pray. Even such a simple thing as grace at meals may have a bad result unless the parents feel the need of the practice, irrespective of the child.

The temptation of parents is to start family prayers, or grace at meals, for the sake of the child. That may be quite all right if it means only that the birth of the child has changed their outlook and led them to see the value of prayer. No doubt this does happen in a great many cases, for a baby can awaken a great sense of wonder and mystery and with them a feeling of responsibility for a being committed to their care, all of which turns the parents away from mutual self-sufficiency to a realization of their dependence on God. This is only to be desired, for then their prayers are genuine.

The temptation I am referring to is that of praying for the sake of the child, with some vague idea that it will be good for him and his development and that it is the right thing to do. In this case the prayers are not really addressed to God, but are aimed at the child, and are inherently hypocritical. The child very soon detects the hypocrisy, and therefore from the beginning he associates religion with hypocrisy, and when he can, he rejects it. Before they can teach their children to pray, parents must first learn themselves to pray, for their own sake.

A similar danger lies in sending children to Sunday school when they themselves do not practise churchgoing. They are in effect telling the children that religion is good for children, but not for grown-ups, and encouraging them to look forward to the time when they may drop it, as their parents have done, who are their real ideal. If the children get interested in religion, however, they will be pulled away from their parents and come to distrust them in other things. Fortunately, however, such children nowadays frequently succeed in persuading their parents to come to church with them, with excellent results.

On the other hand, if non-churchgoing parents try to keep their children away from church or Sunday school, they create another conflict in those cases where the playmates of their children go, for then their children feel that they are out of the swim. As the social instincts grow stronger from three years onwards, this social pull can be a strong one, and not to be doing what their associates are doing can create a sense of inferiority, frustration, and even resentment in them. If non-believing parents send their children to church, they should allow themselves to be persuaded to go with them, simply for the sake of social or family unity. The children do not see this as hypocrisy, because the parents have not initiated it, but are responding to the children.

Trust in their parents and the sense of sharing with them is the most important factor in the healthy development of children in all ways, and it is more likely to lead to future religious strength than any teaching given in these early years. If there is no social pressure to imitate their playmates it is better for the children of non-believers to have no religious training at all in this period. The very strength they have gained from unity with their parents may enable them at a later point to break away from them and turn to religion without losing respect for them.

The case is different where we are dealing with the children of regular churchgoers. Parents have to sacrifice many things for the sake of their children, but it is not right, nor is it good for the children, that they should give up trying to live their own lives just because they are burdened with the care of the children. Churchgoers cannot be expected to give up the habits of worship they had formed, although they may have to modify them in the new circumstances. There are practical difficulties, of course, for the mother of a young baby, particularly when the baby becomes mobile and is not yet able to understand or take part in group activities. Because most households cannot afford a nursemaid, unless reliable baby-sitters are available Father and Mother have to take turns between minding the baby and going to church.

Many churches have opened up crèches and nursery departments at the time of the morning services to look after the young children while the parents are in church. Up to the age of three, the work in these consists simply in watching over the baby and keeping it amused if awake. Children of three and over begin to need group activities, and to many people this seems an opportunity for beginning religious instruction. What should be its aim, and what form should it take?

The danger is of assuming without reflection that they must be taught religion, because they are at a religious centre and their parents are at the time engaged in religious activities. This assumption is easy to understand. The church buildings are used almost exclusively for religious gatherings of one kind or another and come to take on an aura of religiosity. It is quite shocking to some people to consider using a church for the production of a 'secular' play, or for the exhibition of 'non-religious' art, or for light music. Classical music seems to be more readily accepted as compatible with religion.

To this point of view, whatever goes on in the church must be 'religious', and since the children are brought together in the church, or one of its buildings, they are there to be taught religion. And this further assumes that the teaching of religion must be direct and that what the children get must be instruction in religious matters.

We must agree with the aim of helping children to grow into religion, but the assumption that this can be done by direct instruction confuses the end with the means. We may teach the children the words and the postures of religion, but we cannot teach them religion until they have passed out of the infantile period. As we have repeatedly seen, any attempt to instruct them in religion as such is more likely to do harm than good. This does not mean that we ignore religion in teaching them. Our aim will still be to lead them forward to religion and we may even teach them the material of religion – indeed, it is a useful thing to do – but we must do so with understanding of what it means to them.

Let us get clear what is happening when young children are brought to church or Sunday school. They come because their parents come. They are not just passive objects, brought to church and put out of the way. They inevitably will be interested in what their parents do and will want to share in it. Since they do not understand the inner meaning of worship, what their parents do means gathering in church, saying certain things, some of which the children can learn to repeat fairly easily, singing hymns, and listening to readings or addresses. They observe this going on and they note it as one of the facts of the world about which they are learning.

Like any other novel thing that comes to their attention, especially anything concerned with their parents, it arouses their interest. They are therefore ready and eager to take part in such activities, provided they are within their comprehension. Their interest is familial and intellectual, not religious, and what they are given to do should be governed by this. That is to say, the teaching given to children in church or Sunday school should be seen as a means of developing the children's grasp of a world in which religion is a normal element. They are sharing in something that goes on around them, or so it seems to them, and they find their own interest in it. This is the way they grow up. Later on, they will discover a new meaning in these things. In the meantime, any attempt to impose a moral or doctrinal purpose on what they are doing diverts them from the healthy line of growth.

The teaching of young children should therefore be governed by two cardinal principles, neither of which is primarily religious. They must be kept interested and enjoy what they are asked to learn or do, and the teaching must be adapted to the stage of their mental development.

They must be kept interested and enjoy their Sunday school or children's service, because the first impressions they form on attending church are likely to be permanently associated with the idea of church and religion. If they are pleasant to begin with, there will be an enduring feeling that religion is something enjoyable. If the first associations are painful and unpleasant, religion will always stand for something to be faced with difficulty.

Of course, some people look on religion as a matter of painful duty, as an obligation to be accepted and carried out, but I cannot accept this as the right understanding of worship at least, which is intended to be a refreshment and a joy, and in which praise and thanksgiving play the leading part. It is wrong to try to impose obligations of a religious nature on little children. The first requisite of a successful Sunday school is that the children should enjoy it, because of the need to create in their mind the idea that religion has to do with happiness, and for them at this infantile stage of understanding, religion means going to church. It is almost irrelevant what they are taught, so long as they are made happy and kept interested; kept interested, because boredom is a terrible enemy to children, and it is not unknown to be bored in church!

We need not go to that extreme, for the materials of religion can be made very interesting to children once the doctrinal and moral emphasis is removed from it. (Perhaps this applies to the teaching of adults also!) The teaching given must be adapted to their mental development. At this stage, we have seen, they are fertile in imagination and have not yet learned to draw a clear distinction between fact and fancy. They are also still thinking largely by means of images and not by abstract ideas and logical inference. They therefore can be told stories almost without limit, and the Bible is an abundant source of stories.

In selecting the stories, it is a mistake to choose them according to what adults think will be 'good' for the children, that is, edifying and leading to a nice moral lesson, or some nice religious sentiment, such as being kind. Children may be left to develop their own judgements, and that will come gradually. The interests of children often surprise the unsuspecting adult. My wife once told a class of young children the story of Moses and the exodus from Egypt. She asked the children to draw something from the story. The majority of the children, who were girls, drew, not Moses in the bulrushes, but Moses slaughtering the Egyptians and burying them!

This did not mean that the storytelling merely taught the children that even murder was justifiable in religion! On the contrary, it enabled the children to bring out an interest that otherwise they might have repressed and therefore helped to poison their minds later, and by bringing it out to make it possible to grow beyond it when other interests superseded it. They were not made to feel wrong because that was their particular interest, but were encouraged to see other things as well.

The stories need to be told simply as stories without any effort to impress them on the children as true or to point any moral lesson. The latter takes away the interest of the children, and makes them suspicious both of the story and of the motives of the storyteller. They feel they are being 'got at', and resent it. They are not being treated as persons.

The art of storytelling needs to be studied carefully by the teacher, for the use of graphic detail is essential in telling stories to children. Details are important to them, for they make the connecting links. For an adult the abstract meaning ties the story together, and details are apt to obscure this. Children live through the story, and detail makes it possible for them to enter into it and absorb it. The story must be told so that they can picture it going on before their eyes in all its colour and movement. They will in that way absorb more of the essence of it than from any moral the teacher may seek to draw. The life of Jesus, the stories he himself told, the doings of the great heroes of religion, can all be passed on to children in this way and become material to help them to grow. But they must be left to absorb the stories in their own way and make their own selection of what is relevant to life.

The span of attention is not very long in little children and they cannot sit still for more than ten minutes or so without action. Action is a mode by which they express themselves and their interest in something. It enables them to absorb it more effectively. They can therefore be encouraged to act out parts of the stories that are told to them, or to re-enact them with the play materials they have to hand: wood blocks, dolls, and so on. No great amount of dramatic talent can be expected from them, nor is it likely that they can in their acting conceive the story as a dramatic whole. They are more likely to be interested in some detail from the story. The acting or the playing is valuable for the stimulation of their imaginations rather than as a performance for onlookers.

Participation in the story is the valuable part. The story must be left to produce its own moral, and the teacher should not be alarmed if in enacting, let us say, the story of the Good Samaritan, more enthusiasm is shown for the part of the thieves or the victim than for the Good Samaritan himself. Nevertheless, by discreet care in making clear the details of what the Samaritan did, it is possible for the teacher to highlight his role without overtly trying to draw any moral from the story.

Children also enjoy singing and dancing games. Unfortunately, there is a great dearth of suitable hymns for little children, or for older children for that matter. Children's hymns, so called, tend to be too pious and sentimental. Even though they will get little meaning from the words of the hymn, it tends to leave an impression of its general tone. Good adult hymns may be used even if the words are beyond the grasp of the children. If need be, the meaning of the words can be explained simply. Usually it is far better to give the children bright and happy nursery songs to sing, without any consideration of their religious import, and these are reasonably plentiful. Similarly in the games they play and in their dances there is no need to look for any special religious flavour. The important thing is to keep the children interested and happy so that they will enjoy their time in class. They can be trusted to work out connexions with religion in their own imaginations.

CHAPTER 14

THE GOODNESS OF THE CHILD

EVERY mother, as well as every father, wants her baby to be a good baby and to grow up and be a good man or woman. She may want other things as well. She may want her baby, if he is a boy, to grow up and be a success in life, be rich or famous; or if she is a girl, to be beautiful, a social success, make a good marriage, and so on. These other wishes for her baby's future are sometimes difficulties in the way of his goodness. That is, she does not desire goodness alone for him. This does not mean that she is insincere in wanting him to be good. It only means that she has not sorted out and integrated her own values in life. This confusion in herself is certain to affect the development of the baby, for he inevitably absorbs some of her outlook on life. Two or more incompatible ideas may pull him in different directions as he grows and create divisions in his personality.

Enduring goodness of life is one of the signs of mature religious development, for it is only possible when belief and action have been brought together into a unity of the spirit. It involves singleness of mind. 'If thine eye be single, thy whole body shall be full of light.' A good man is at one with himself, and his actions reveal the unity of his inner personality. This unity is the result of a long process of growth, which begins from birth and which involves every aspect of the personality, the mind, and the emotions as well as the actions.

As in everything else to do with religion, the foundations of goodness are laid in infancy. We saw in the earlier part of this book that, until he passes from infancy, somewhere in the years after the age of five, the young child has no moral sense like that of the adult. He gets that only by growing through infancy. The moral sense by which we distinguish between right and wrong is not inborn; it has to be acquired by growth in the environment of the family. Right and wrong have meanings for the infant that are different from those that they have for the adult. In the adult, conscience and a sense of obligation to do what is judged to be right are the ultimate motives and controls on conduct. The infant is moved by other forces. These other forces are the raw materials out of which his moral sense is shaped, and the way they develop depends on the way he is treated by his parents, especially by his mother in the first two years, for on her the main burden falls in starting the child on the way to goodness.

The stages by which a moral sense is attained are complicated, as we have already seen, and there is plenty of opportunity for the development to go astray. The crux of the matter may be put simply enough; the problem is to carry out in practice the precepts that issue from it. It is this: standards of behaviour do not have to be imposed upon the child from without by the training that is given to the child, as clothing is put upon his body. He has to be helped to form his own standards by a process of inner growth. Training may help him to form these standards, but sometimes it hinders, if it is the wrong sort of training. The standards he attains to may be those of his parents or they may be different ones. The important thing is that parents should recognize that moral training does not consist in moulding him by whatever means are possible to their preconceived pattern of behaviour, which they will be very tempted to do, if only because of the child's apparent helplessness and immaturity, and because he is theirs. Instead, it consists in helping him to become himself. The help and guidance of his parents is essential to this development, but they must cooperate with the powers that are working from within the child, adapting their help to each stage of his growth.

The child is not a passive piece of material that can be moulded at will, but is a living organism, endowed with powerful dispositions and appetites, and what he becomes will depend upon the way the influences from outside him meet the forces working from within. It is futile and even harmful to set up an idea in advance and to say, 'That is what I am going to make my child.' Children cannot be brought up according to a book of rules and working to a timetable. They cannot be brought up at all. They grow up. They grow up in the context of their environment, the family situation, and they have a large contribution to make to that situation. They are not passive; they are active members of the family.

It will help us to see our way more clearly if we recall what is the nature of the moral sense that is the final result of the development during the first seven years of life. We saw that the child emerges from infancy with an inner standard of conduct, which we loosely call conscience, because it incorporates an inner authority on moral questions, questions affecting right or wrong. It imposes an unquestioned obligation to do what is right and avoid what is wrong, once we recognize it. We saw, too, that there is some difference between the way this authority works in boys and girls. Conscience is only a loose name for it, for this inner function of the mind concerns itself with more than the moral standards that we associate with conscience. In other words, this new activity of the mind is a complex one, bringing together various mental processes, and there is no one name completely suitable to describe it. It is therefore all the more important in the upbringing of children that we should consider separately the various strands that go to make it, so that we can try to foster those that will contribute most in sharing a good life. It also helps us to clear our minds about what we mean by goodness.

In tracing the growth of the moral sense of conscience, we saw that the child emerges with two aspects of it: one that forbids him to do that which he has come to accept as wrong, the other that encourages and urges him to do that which he knows as right. The words 'right' and 'wrong' are here also used loosely, not with any reference to absolute standards of right and wrong, if such exist, but simply relative to what the child has come to associate with them as their meaning. Confusion arises if we think that the two judgements or the two impulses are from exactly the same source. They are not. They represent separate lines of development, even if they come to be linked together.

We can put it this way: to learn what is wrong does not always teach us what is right, for the alternatives to one wrong action may include a great many other wrong actions; and even when the right action is known, it does help the child to *desire* to do the right action by forbidding the wrong. The parent who is continually saying 'Don't do that' is not helping the child to do what is right. Every child needs to be helped to act positively as well as to be able to refrain from wrong action. A little girl once put it very clearly to me when she said, 'I know what I ought to do, but I don't know how to want to do it.' She was an exceptionally intelligent girl, able to make this analysis of herself, but what she was able to express consciously is the state of most small children. They need the help of their parents to enable them to want to do what is right and good.

Within each child are two forces that are the mainspring of his positive moral development, two forces that should work together if they are to achieve the right result. They are, first, the child's sense of order or meaning, and second, his love for his mother (I am now thinking of the first two years), which shows itself in his desire to share all his experiences with her in an intimate personal relationship. Too much must not be read into this last phrase, for he is not at first aware of himself and his mother as separate persons. What the child desires is to bring every experience into association with that central group of happy experiences that is his mother, so that it gets a heightened value from the link with the good mother.

The sense of order to which I have referred is not to be understood as the neatness and tidiness most mothers desire their children to have, and into which they try to train them. It is the urge the human mind has to group perceptions into patterns: patterns of sound, patterns of form and colour, patterns of movement, patterns involving all these at once and, finally, patterns of meaning. Disorder and chaos are the negation of pattern, and the mind is constantly trying to bring order into chaos. Art, music, dancing, thinking, all are different forms of pattern-making that grow out of the urge to order. So too is morality. In morality the individual act is fitted into the pattern of the ideal, or rejected from it, which is another way of relating to it the ideal. The child is struggling from the moment of birth to create such patterns out of the isolated experiences he undergoes. He is predisposed to be moral.

His need for the love of his mother and an active personal relationship with her, which is the most important element in his life, predisposes him in turn to accept her guidance as far as he is able to interpret it from her actions. He knows when she is pleased with him, when angry. He wants to please her, but his capacity to do so is limited by his immaturity. He has not acquired any great mastery over all the impulses that are natural to him. Self-control comes only gradually. If the mother asks too much of him, asks him to do something that is not yet in his power and shows disappointment or anger when he does not succeed, she puts a sharp tension into him between his desire to please her and his inability to do so. By trying to hurry up his development she puts a strain on him that endangers that development. There is one crucial instance of this that may have considerable effect on his moral growth, namely, the supposed training of the baby in the orderly evacuation of his bladder and bowels.

It is important for the child's moral development how the mother trains her child in 'cleanliness'. It is a much more fundamental matter than personal hygiene and maternal convenience. The word 'training' is likely to mislead her into trying to impose her desires, her conception of what is proper, on her baby, and to believe that it is only by her teaching that the baby is brought to ordered habits. She may in consequence overlook the more important fact that within him there is a developing urge to control that is not simply a desire to please his mother, although that is there too, but is natural to him.

We can compare the process with his feeding at the breast. At first all that the baby seems to want is food when he is at the breast. Very soon he begins to show signs of pleasure with his hands, fondling the breast, and perhaps continuing to keep the nipple in his mouth after he has taken all that he needs. Then he shows signs of anticipation of pleasure over and above his hunger, and before long he will enjoy a period of playing with the breast and looking at his mother before he begins to suck. He is learning to control his hunger desire, to wait for the appropriate moment before satisfying it. There is something he enjoys more than the immediate satisfaction of his appetite; it is the communion with his mother.

This is made possible to him because his mother has likewise enjoyed the feeding and has shown her pleasure to her baby. It was a shared experience, and so not only satisfied the baby's hunger but also satisfied that more fundamental need, the need to love and be loved and to experience an intimate personal relationship. It is this that gives him the power to control his natural appetite. It is taken in a wider setting of a satisfying mental or spiritual communion with his mother.

The baby expects to get the same personal relationship from the evacuation of his bladder and bowels. This to him is a pleasant and comforting function that he also wants to share with his mother. He expects her to get the same pleasure from his evacuation as he does. At first she does appear to enjoy it with him and to praise him for his performance. The situation is apt to change too soon for the baby.

In this respect the mother comes up against her own inhibitions and standards, which all too often amount almost to an obsession. She has acquired a distaste for uncleanness, and particularly for excrement, which the baby has not yet developed. She wants her baby to be clean for the sake of cleanliness rather than for his sake, and, in consequence, she is liable to try to push him on too fast. In subservience to her own psychological need, she makes demands on him that he is unable to fulfil. He simply has not the power to control his evacuations. When his mother expresses or even feels disappointment with him for his failure, and above all when she does not recognize his signs of distress and cooperate with him when he needs to evacuate, she disappoints him and he feels that he has disappointed her.

What should have been an occasion of shared pleasure and a growing together of mother and baby is wasted, and more than wasted, for it has become an occasion of deep disappointment and a sense of failure. If, however, the mother is patient and does not try to hurry the baby into self-control faster than he can grow into it, their relationship in this matter can be a source of moral strength to him. He learns self-control because of his love for his mother and because the self-control is built into a full sharing of experience with her.

This is not morality yet, but it is a beginning, since self-control and redirection of the natural impulses are an essential part of morality. At this early stage the word 'good' means to the baby only what pleases his mother, plus the overtone of satisfaction that comes to him when he is able to set his action – feeding, evacuation, play, and so on – into the context of sharing it with her. She calls him a 'good' baby when he does what she wants him to do, which he usually wants to do also, and the adjective has no special moral significance. He is 'good' when he takes his food well, when he sleeps, when he goes down quietly, smiles in response to her play with him, and so on.

This is as it should be. He can understand these things, but he cannot make moral judgements. There is thus set up in his mind the ideal of pleasing her as the meaning of goodness, and badness is to do that which displeases her. There are other things that are bad, the pains that he suffers from wind, or hurts, or other sources, and also the uncontrollable impulses to which he is subjected: fierce hunger that makes him want to attack and swallow his mother, the frustrations he has to undergo at times, and the rages that threaten to shake him to pieces. We have already seen how these affect his development. What we are tracing now is the way in which his positive ideal of good conduct is formed and the forces that give it strength.

Out of the desire to do what pleases his mother he forms two things. First, he forms an ideal of his mother so that she lives in his mind or imagination, as it were, as a means by which to shape his desires. She does not need always to be physically present. He can share with her in imagination and anticipation, and control his desires accordingly. Second, he forms a picture of himself as always doing what she wants, that is, a picture of himself as he thinks she desires him to be. He knows that he falls short of this frequently, but he desires to be this ideal self, so that he may go on enjoying unbroken his satisfying personal relationship with her. Here is the first division between his real and his ideal self, between what he actually does and what, for the sake of her love, he wants to do or not do.

The next stage of his development, when the father comes into his awareness as a separate person, gives this ideal self a new boost, but at the same time alters its character. The boy sees in his father an ideal of what he wants to become, big, wise, all-capable. He not only wants to do what his father tells him and what he believes will please his father; he wants also to become like his father, and this is a powerful motive to fashion his thinking and his conduct – the most powerful, if the child is wisely handled. Similarly, the girl wants to become like her mother and not only do things to please her. There are also cross-currents that lead the boy to want to be like his mother and the girl like her father, but these are subsidiary to the others and we need not pursue them for separate treatment.

In this stage, too, we see that the ideal of the self that is formed is not primarily a moral one, but rather a personal or social one. The child wants to be like his parent, not because he judges the latter to be good – he has no other standards by which to judge – but because it seems the most desirable thing, and this ideal becomes a lodestone directing the lines of his growth. When at a later point this ideal is transformed into a moral ideal, and this happens in healthy development, it provides the most powerful force making for a positive morality. This morality is not governed by fear of consequences, but is a fulfilment of the self. It is the self becoming what it most desires to be. We shall see that in the later stages of his growth the original image-ideal of the parent becomes enlarged to take in other heroes, other models of conduct, until in the end God becomes that which the moral self most aspires after.

Before we take up that later development we must look at the negative aspect of the conscience, the aspect that is concerned with forbidding us to do wrong. It will simplify the exposition if we refer to this aspect of conscience as the superego, calling the positive aspect the ego-ideal.

We traced the origins of the superego in the first section of this book, and it is enough here to recall only the main points established there. The superego begins in the first few months of life as a division within the aggressive instincts whereby part of the aggression is turned inwards upon the self to restrain destructive impulses directed towards the mother, or, more precisely, towards her breast. These grow into wider aggressive impulses as the mother becomes more of a whole person to the child. The aggression is then stirred up not only by frustrations in feeding or natural greed; it is called into activity by any kind of frustration or thwarting, whether intentional or not, when the baby cannot get what it wants and no substitute is provided to divert its desires.

Two things follow. Because a function of self-attack or self-criticism has been set up in the child's mind, he feels himself to be bad. Second, there is also formed in his mind the image of a bad or hostile mother, for his frustrations and sufferings are ascribed to her. This is inevitable, since he knows nothing else but her. Corresponding to the double mother image, he himself is divided into two, into good and bad, and this division is confirmed by his experience. When he grows sufficiently in understanding, he is able to realize that his mother is apt to call him bad and appear to withdraw her love from him when he is doing or has done something that displeases her. (I am here speaking of what commonly happens rather than of what ought to happen. Mothers should be reluctant to call their children bad and threaten not to love them if they do this or that.) The child comes to think that badness lies, then, in being hostile and in provoking the displeasure of the hostile mother.

Similarly, in the next stage of development, the father appears in two guises: as the good father to be admired and emulated, the model of behaviour (or, in the case of the girl, to be loved and obeyed and possessed), and as the bad father, the powerful rival for the mother's love, who threatens dire punishment if the young child does not give up his desire for his mother. This we called the crisis of infancy, and we saw that the way forward was by the introjection of the parent image to form a conscience, the so-called superego, with the ego-ideal attached to it. The savagery of the self-directed aggressive instincts is taken into it to give it more force. The child at this stage has become a moral being, with an inner standard of judgement and a sense of obligation to do what his conscience tells him is right and to refrain from what it says is wrong. This conscience is the voice in him of the combined parent image, which has become part of his mind and personality.

The first standards this conscience imposes are those taken over with the parent image and the self-directed aggression. They are concerned with the things that were displeasing to the parents and brought him into the danger of losing their love, and with those emotions which by their violence threatened the disruption of the self even when they did not bring immediate danger from the world. Thus in this negative superego aspect conscience operates from fear: fear of loss of love, fear of displeasing the parents or the parent symbols, fear of punishment, fear of being destroyed. The sources of those fears were almost always certain strong desires: love desires and hate desires, desire to swallow the breast or bite it off, desire to play with excrement, desire to play with the sensitive genital organs, desire (in the later stages) to possess the mother in as sexual a way as the child can understand; and hatred of the mother for frustrating various desires and compelling unpleasant things, and hatred of the father for his possession of the mother.

This negative aspect produces by inversion what is sometimes mistaken for positive goodness, a sense of duty. If we are to avoid losing love we must do those (usually) difficult and unpleasant things the parent image within us prescribes. As in babyhood, so in later life that usually means giving up things we enjoy, the natural lusts and pleasures, and doing things for which we have little natural inclination. This is the attitude of many religious people, typified in the so-called 'Puritan conscience'. Many of the things prescribed by it may be very good, but the fear motive that inspires such a conscience is not really positive at all. It must not be confused with the freedom and joy that characterize a life governed by a well-formed ego-ideal: '. . . who for the *joy* that was set before him endured the cross, despising the shame . . .' (Hebrews, 12: 2).

These are the foundations on which religion will be built. Because in religion God will take the place of the parent image, it becomes important which aspect of the parents is most strongly developed in the child in this first part of his life. If it is the bad father image that is predominant – and the father image takes up into it the corresponding mother image – any idea of God that is later developed will be a fear God, an enemy God, watching always to catch out the offender and to give dire punishment, a God who takes the joy and pleasure out of living but exacts unswerving obedience.

Religion founded on such a God is a religion of duty and propitiation by sacrifice. If the predominant parent image formed in infancy is of the good parent, the God who develops out of it will be a God of Love, one who is to be loved in return, not out of duty but because he is lovable, a God who is a giver and enricher of life, who forgives sins because he is anxious to lead his children forward, a God with whom there can be fellowship.

This distinction between good and bad parents refers, of course, to two strands that will be found in the same person, so that in all relationships between parent and child there is a mixture of both. It obviously is desirable that the good parent image should be the dominant one, and this can be brought about only by the mother in particular sharing the growing experience of the child in the positive way. Attempts to impose training and discipline beyond the capacity of the child to bear it lead inevitably to the bad image. So too does any attempt to teach about God at an early age, for the young child is unable to enter into any direct fellowship with God. Teaching about God and his commandments should be deferred until the child is thoroughly established in personal security and has learned from his parents that the world is a loving one rather than an enemy one.

One further point needs to be added before we end this account of the growth of the infant towards the understanding of what goodness is and its actualization in his behaviour. The child emerges from infancy with his two-ways conscience. This has been formed out of his struggle to grow through the experiences, the fears and anxieties, the disappointments, and the joys of infancy, and to master his relations with his father and mother at the successive stages of his growth.

This new organ of judgement does not operate in a vacuum, able to discern right and wrong, good and bad, in any situation that may confront the child. It implements the standards it has inherited from infancy, and in any new situation that arises it works only by measuring it against those infantile standards and with the infantile point of view. It interprets the new situation in terms of the old. If, as easily happens, God takes the place of the parent image, his supposed commandments are accepted by conscience as obligatory, and they may be interpreted in an infantile way, without any effort to question them or to see more deeply into their meaning.

In other words, conscience needs to be educated, both in its positive and negative aspects. It has to grow so that the development in moral standards keeps pace with the other aspects of the child's growth. That other growth is towards realism and independence. The development of the moral sense must take the same line. The authority the parents naturally possess over him should give way gradually to the moral self-dependence of the child, and their function come to be that of advisers and enlighteners rather than directors or controllers; they will give information rather than orders.

This means that quite early the parents should begin to give reasons for what they ask the child to do, reasons of course that the child can at least partly understand, practical reasons based on the cause and effect of actions. They will rely less and less on the child's fear of losing their love as the dominant motive in his behaviour, and they will begin to give the words 'good' and 'bad' a much wider meaning than they first had with him. In this way they help him to turn his young conscience away from his own fears and his preoccupation with his parents out to the world at large, and they lead his growth towards the universalizing of conscience. Unless this happens, his conscience will operate effectively only in the limited field of his own family or substitutes for the family: his friends, class, nation.

This process of fostering moral autonomy and a universal conscience cannot be hurried; it must be gradual. It imposes too great a burden on a young child to ask him to make profound moral decisions at every turn, when he has neither the knowledge nor the experience on which to base them. The aim of parents and educators must be to steer their way between complete authoritarianism, which keeps the conscience infantile, and the withdrawal of all guidance, which asks too much of him, and equally handicaps his growth.

The child's conscience is only part of him, and if he is to grow to maturity it must grow along with the rest of him into the ultimate integrated self. It is part of him, and must not be set over against him as an independent controlling force, a superego. His goodness must be the expression not only of the standards his conscience serves but also of his whole personality.

CHAPTER 15

THE YEARS OF CONSOLIDATION

WE have contended that the foundations of religious life are laid in the first seven years and that they are laid by the treatment given to the child during those years, not by any religious instruction that may be attempted. Direct religious education is premature and may result in so arresting the development of the child that he cannot pass through the phases necessary to his free growth. If, however, the child has been led successfully through this period, the building may now begin upon the foundations.

For the sake of simplicity we shall refer to this next period after the passage of infancy as childhood. It ends with the onset of puberty at about the age of thirteen, when adolescence begins. Freud called this the period of latency, when he was concentrating on tracing the development of the sexual instincts from infancy through to adulthood, because infancy and adolescence are periods of rapid development and of great activity of the sexual (in the wide sense used by Freud) instincts, whereas childhood is a period of calm and stability by comparison, almost as if the body and the psyche were gathering strength for the great uprush of adolescence.

The term 'latency' has proved a little misleading, for it was taken by some to mean that sexual interests disappear, which is not the case, any more than they disappear when the sexual instincts have reached their full development and stability in adulthood. In the latency period there is no further development of the forms in which they express themselves, bodily or mentally.

A more fruitful suggestion is that referred to earlier, made by the great psychoanalyst Dr Ernest Jones, the biographer of Freud, who pointed out that childhood is like a first adulthood. Man is distinguished from the lower animals by growing up twice. The latter pass from birth to maturity on one smooth sweep of growth, but man's development is interrupted. In childhood a certain degree of maturity is reached, but this is broken up by the great upheaval – bodily, mentally, emotionally – of adolescence. Thus there is closer affinity between childhood and adulthood than between childhood and infancy. Adolescence is a kind of second infancy, in which development is rapid as in the first infancy and there is a similar richness of imagination and fantasy. Childhood, on the other hand, is a period of stability and toughness, a period of consolidation rather than of change.

Infancy, we saw, developed to a sharp emotional crisis that was overcome by the internalization of the parent image to form the superego and ego-ideal, by means of which the child was enabled to let go his sensuous emotional attachments to his parents. This sets him free to turn away from them towards the outside world, and it is towards that that his energies are now directed. He has to begin to find his place in it as an individual and to test out his developing powers on it.

He proceeds to investigate it, to learn to manipulate the things he finds in it, and to measure himself against the other people who belong to it. He begins to see his parents as part of a much bigger world, and one of the first tasks is to get an objective appraisal of them. They cease to be the focus of the world to him. As an infant he saw and reacted to the world through his attachment to his parents; now he begins to see his parents through the outside world. This requires an adjustment of outlook, which takes place rapidly, if gradually.

He has carried over from infancy images of his parents that no longer fit them. Those images were formed under the influence of his emotional dependence on them, and the goodness or badness, and the greatness, of his parents as he saw them corresponded more to his emotional needs than to the reality. He can now look more objectively at his parents, and his emotional attachments are not so intense as they were in infancy; he is able to see them more as they are, to compare them with other people and even with himself, and bit by bit he reduces them to the human scale. The memory of godlike creatures remains in his mind, even if it is at the unconscious level, waiting to be reactivated when a suitable occasion arises: in love, in hero-worship, or in religion, for example.

Parallel with the mental and emotional turning away from the family and the increased interest in the outside world that goes with it, there is also an increase in the need for action. The energies of the mind are not absorbed in inner conflict and change, as they were in infancy, but find their outlet in bodily and mental activity of all kinds. In this period of childhood children are almost inexhaustible, and the fertility of their devisings is almost beyond the capacity of an adult to keep pace with it.

This is particularly true of their gang play, for this is the age when boys – and girls, to a lesser extent – consort with their mates in gangs, in which they test out their capacity for leadership and for obedience to the group leader who emerges in their play. They learn the meaning of loyalty and group unity or *esprit de corps*. Individual rivalries have to be subordinated to the unity of the group, and the codes of conduct of the group become the controlling standards of behaviour. The individual is being fashioned into a member of society in which his personal adjustments go beyond the family, in which his personal life was first moulded into shape. Although this means bursting through the family limitations, it is possible only because of what he had become by his development in the family.

With the onset of childhood he is now ready to face up

to religion proper and to begin to come to grips directly with the ideas and practices of religion. If he has progressed satisfactorily through infancy, it is now safe to teach him about God; indeed, he needs this teaching. Any such teaching should, however, take account of the psychological characteristics of childhood outlined above, if it is to have its full result.

It is of no use to expect a child to assimilate teaching that postulates emotional susceptibility and introspectiveness of the kind we find in the period of adolescence. It is true that some children may be unstable, but that is because they have not succeeded in growing completely out of infancy.

We are here trying to follow out the development of the normal healthy child. He is consolidating himself in the world during this period, and he is naturally interested in everything that he meets in the world. This includes the religious ideas and practices that form part of his environment. He approaches them objectively and critically, testing them as he tests everything he encounters. Childhood is very much a period of learning, in which the mind is industriously accumulating miscellaneous information by observation or instruction, sorting it, storing it, digesting it.

The possibilities of religious development in childhood must be understood in the light of these main characteristics of the period. Looking at it first from the point of view of the interior development of the child's mind, we see that his chief task is to relate what he has carried over from infancy to the world outside himself and also outside the family circle. It involves the struggle to discover reality, and one of the first lines of development is to find the means of discriminating between reality, what he calls 'true' things, and 'fairy stories', or 'make-believe', and so on. He has to find a reality basis for what he has learned to cherish.

For instance, the truth or otherwise of Santa Claus becomes an issue of great interest. To discover that Santa Claus is only the parents does not rob the Christmas gifts and surprises of their emotional value; it probably strengthens and enhances their value by adding to it the element of family love that is expressed in them. The child is quite willing for a time to go on pretending to believe in Santa Claus, but he derives additional enjoyment from the secret feeling of knowing the truth. The possession of knowledge is a great satisfaction and reinforcement of the sense of being an individual person. It also heightens the sense of power or control over the world.

The idea of God, in whatever form he has carried it over from infancy, is subjected to similar testing. The difficulty for the child is that God cannot be brought under direct observation of any kind. It is at this point that the child needs the right kind of teaching, and where the importance of the foundations laid in infancy becomes apparent. If the 'bad father' image of God has become the dominant one, the task of testing him out in reality may be too frightening, as well as too arduous, and the child will be liable to tuck away his idea of God into the unconscious recesses of his mind and give up the effort to relate this God to truth and reality as he is discovering it in other spheres of his thinking. God will remain in the realm of 'fairy story'. A friend of mine with whom I was discussing this point a couple of years ago (before the first space flights) told me that one morning as she was following two of her grandsons, aged about seven and eight, away from church and Sunday school she heard the older say to the younger, 'I believe it is true what they told us in there about Jesus, but I know there isn't a God. Why, they haven't even got a man into space yet!' This is a most revealing comment showing, first, how directly children interpret the idea of God when it is presented to them, and, second, how ideas at this age are subjected to the test of practical reality. If God cannot stand up to the test, he is not real.

The later consequences may well be that in adolescence or adulthood the child will have gained the courage to throw overboard this 'unreal' God, becoming an atheist or agnostic. If he does not follow this course, it is likely that the God in whom he believes will have little relation to the everyday world and the ordinary events of life, except to stand over and above them as a threatening despot whose fiats have always an aspect of arbitrariness and hostility in them. His religion will be in a separate compartment from the rest of his life.

Even in the case of the atheist the rejection of God is not always successful, for the infantile image of him persists in the unconscious and renders its possessor a ready victim to other kinds of authority. This lies at the heart of communism, where the father image is projected on to the current boss of the party.

It is not easy to judge whether a young child has formed his first idea of God out of the image of the 'bad' father. If he has, he is likely to shrink from it, to hide it, and avoid facing it. Sometimes it will manifest itself by the kind of tentative questions he asks about God, or in severe cases, by his not asking. Or it may show itself by a refusal to go to church or Sunday school, for which refusal questionable reasons are advanced. But such behaviour may result from other motives. We can assume that in every child there is some admixture of the 'bad' father in his idea of God, which he must learn to face and overcome. This is best done indirectly, by treatment and teaching that enable him to develop the 'good' father element.

The development of the 'good' father image of God will have two component elements, the realistic and the moral. The realistic will come from the urge to test out the idea of God that he has carried over from infancy and as it is presented to him in his current experience by parents or teachers, or picked up from discussions with other children.

The child wants to find a God who works and produces manifest results, such as clear answers to prayer. Many a child has his faith shaken in the God he is told about when that God fails to produce a direct answer to the requests the child makes to him. On the other hand, God can be invoked as the maker of the universe and the controller of events, always provided, of course – and this is very important – that as the child comes to understand natural law and the principles of causation, God is shown as working through these and not as a substitute for them. That is to say, the teaching about God must be graduated to the child's understanding of the world, so that there is progressive expansion of the idea of God, and the child's religious understanding keeps pace with his growth in knowledge in other matters. Further, the teaching about God should be related to his other knowledge as far as is possible.

In this way the infantile expectation of a magical answer to prayer – an answer of which the child is afraid because it would deny the reality principle that is now so important to him – is gradually dissolved and its place taken by the realization that God works through the ordinary channels of people and events. The way is prepared for this by factual teaching about religion. To this we shall return in a few moments.

The second component element in this development consists of the widening of the child's moral conceptions. The end of infancy saw the development of a moral sense. This took over the standards of conduct developed within the family, both positive and negative, that sprang out of the desire to please the parents or avoid their anger and to win their love. The part of the parents and the family is now taken by the various groups to which the child belongs.

The extent of the influence of the respective groups depends to a large extent on the strength of the ties that bind the child to the group, that is, on how far the parent image can be transferred to the leader of the group and on how far the child can identify himself with the leader, make him for the time being the expression of his ego-ideal. Where these are strong the child incorporates the rules of the group into his moral sense and they become binding on him.

Where there is conflict between rules of conduct that come from different groups demanding his loyalty, the child can be placed in a very difficult dilemma, finding it hard to choose the right line of behaviour. Should he, for instance, follow his gang into something his parents have told him is wrong? Should he carry tales to his teacher about one of his mates? Problems such as these are acute moral problems for the child, just because he has not yet fought his way through to one overriding set of moral principles or found one all-absorbing loyalty.

We should perhaps note at this point that the girl here develops differently from the boy, because of the fact, noted earlier, that she does not pass out of infancy with the same sort of moral sense as the boy. Girls are not so prone to form gangs as are boys, or to feel the same passionate loyalty to a group. They tend rather to belong to small coteries, with strong bonds among three or four, or even to remain with one 'bosom friend'.

Identification with each other, rather than the transference of the unconscious parent image, seems to govern the ties between girls. They are therefore less ready to take into themselves as clear-cut rules of conduct the rules governing the behaviour of a group, and are, in consequence, much more individual in their morality. Their method of arriving at the right thing to do in a given situation is by projecting themselves into it, identifying themselves with the central figure, rather than applying accepted codes to it.

The interior development of children cannot be separated in practice from what is brought to bear upon them from outside, whether deliberately or unwittingly. The interior responds to the exterior and requires it for its proper unfolding. If they are to be helped to grow religiously, the teaching given them should take full account of these trends of inner growth. The child will absorb only those elements of it that correspond to his mental interests; on the other hand, it is to his subsequent advantage to have his mind stretched along the lines of his natural growth.

That perhaps is the first point we should emphasize about the religious training of children in this period. They are more likely to be given too little than too much information. They can stand up to hard work of the right sort. Since they are busy amassing knowledge about the world outside themselves and have moved away from introspection, they are capable of absorbing a great deal of objective information about religious matters. It needs to be factual and concerned with action as much as possible, with the aim of teaching the child the contents of the Bible, the history of its formation, what the Church believes by way of doctrine, what the various services of the Church mean. All this needs to be graduated to what the child can understand. Provided it can be linked up to his own situation, he can take any amount of information.

It is an error, however, to try to use the information given to him as a basis for moralization and exhortations to be 'good'. His interest is intellectual and factual rather than emotional and ethical. Similarly, he will be alienated if too much effort is put into attempts to impose the teaching on the basis of authority, for this runs counter to his dominant need to examine everything for himself and test its reality value. And emphasis on the rightness of this or that belief is also likely to make him suspicious, because it puts pressure on him to accept it before he has put it to the test himself. The teaching that is given to him should therefore be in the form of 'this is what happened, to the best of our knowledge', or 'this is what the Church teaches, because it is trying to understand and follow Christ'.

Idealism and abstract ideas make no appeal in childhood; they belong to the next period. But heroism does have a great interest, especially for boys, because they are looking for leadership in action. It is easy enough to depict Jesus, the Old Testament prophets, and the saints of the ages in this guise, and their teaching that made them outstanding can be presented as part of the story. It is then absorbed naturally and incidentally, whereas if the same teaching is given as a moral lesson the child is prone to react from it as an attempt by parents or teachers to fetter his new-found freedom of mind.

Before leaving the period of childhood, we should consider the question of attendance at church or Sunday school. No general rules can be laid down to cover all cases, because of the extent to which circumstances differ. There is still an emotional significance attached to going to church with the family, especially in the earlier years of childhood, but because the child is turning away from the family to the world he may want to break away from the family. This means that he may not wish to go *with* the family, that is, with the parents and younger children, walking with them and sitting with them, as he did when he was younger, but would rather go with and to his own group in the church or Sunday school.

This is a sign of his growing independence, and the services and classes should be so arranged that this gradual separation of the family units is provided for. Going to church with the family then means going to the same place as the family – where church and Sunday school are seen as part of the same unit – and going at approximately the same time. It is not always practicable to have the children's classes and worship conducted at the same time as the church services, but where it is possible it is preferable to the older system of having the children in the afternoons only.

If the parents do not attend church, they need not be surprised if the children lose interest in going, because the abstention of the parents is likely to create in the children's minds the idea that church going is not for adults, but something for children and that it is a sign of having grown up to deny the value of going to church or Sunday school. It is also likely to create a problem for the children, too hard for them to solve, in that the parents send their children to church, usually saying that it is good for them, but they themselves decline this good thing. If children go to church without their parents and see other children's parents there, they almost invariably try to persuade their own to attend, revealing their need for the unity of the family.

Conflict of course can be set up in another way. The parents may be regular churchgoers and want their children to attend, but the gangs to which the latter belong may not do so. Gang loyalty is a powerful motive and a factor in the growth through childhood, so when such a situation arises the parents should try to find some way round it other than a straight-out struggle of loyalties. What is possible depends on the individuals concerned. It may be that the children in question can be grafted into another gang. Or the situation may be presented as a challenge to leadership, proved by getting the gang to go to church. Or again, the way out may be found by the interest aroused by the actual teaching given at church.

In every instance account should be taken of the child's need to grow away from his family as a stage on the way to his independence. If pressure has to be exercised to make the child attend, some compensatory freedom should be devised as a proof that the parents are aware that the child is no longer an infant, but has a real measure of responsibility.

The greatest danger to the child is boredom. Church services may be too long, too obscure, and too lacking in action for young children, so that attendance at them is little short of torture. In that case, churchgoing comes to be regarded as a most unpleasant occupation. Very many choirboys develop this attitude, unless their interest is captured in other ways, and leave church as soon as their voices break, simply because they have found the services apart from their singing too incomprehensible to hold their attention. Similarly, the lessons in Sunday school may not be good enough to stretch their minds as they need to be stretched, or so pious and full of moralizing as to have no interest for them, and again boredom is the result, and boredom is very hard for children to bear. Fortunately, most of the churches have awakened to this risk in recent years, and some excellent syllabuses are now available and are being used widely.

Once the attention of children is captured and held, their growing independence fostered and their minds challenged, the period of childhood can be one of strong growth, preparing the way to the final transmutation in adolescence and adulthood.

CHAPTER 16

ADOLESCENCE

ADOLESCENCE is a second period of rapid change within the personality, and for this reason has been likened to a second infancy. The resemblance is more than a superficial one. The first infancy gave time for the mind to take shape and develop the mechanisms by which to make contact with the world surrounding it – the ideas, images, perceptions, interests, memories, habits, by which the infant gradually builds a knowledge of the world – and to develop a system of desires and aversions out of his primitive instinctive impulses. Adolescence, the second infancy, prepares him to take his place in that world and make his life there as a separate and relatively independent individual. For that he has to undergo deep-seated emotional adjustments, by which he acquires a new outlook, accepts new responsibilities, and takes his place as an equal among men, putting the subordinate role of childhood behind him.

Between the two infancies lies the period of consolidation, childhood proper. This pause in childhood is biologically and socially necessary. Man has evolved a very complex society, and a long period of learning is needed for those who would take their place in it. Hence this form of society could be produced only when the innate constitution of man changed from that of his animal forebears and gave him this period of intellectual development and consolidation before society makes its full demands upon him. Simple instinct could not provide for all the contingencies of human life. It needs to be directed by intelligence, using understanding and experience of the world as a guide. So nature provides the interval needed for this, before the work of growing up, which was begun in infancy, is completed in adolescence. After the pause, adolescence takes up the growth that was begun in infancy.

Adolescence begins with puberty, when the sexual glands begin to come to their full development and make the male capable of begetting and the female of bearing a child. The bodily changes that constitute the secondary sexual characteristics inevitably make the adolescent conscious of his body, particularly as there is associated with these changes a strong uprush of new feelings and new interests. The emotional life is greatly enriched, and seeks to move in new directions. The old ways, the former interests, are no longer adequate to provide the channels of expression needed. The personality has to reshape itself under the impetus of the new developments. The stability of childhood gives way to gawkiness and uncertainty until the adolescent period settles down into a permanent shape and merges into the stability of adulthood.

We can follow more easily what is happening in the mind of the adolescent if we see him in the light of these two principles of interpretation; first, that he is growing into full independence in obedience to the innate law of his nature; and second, that the energy to complete this growth is supplied by the physiological changes that come with adolescence, energy in such abundance that it compels him to find new modes of behaviour.

He does not have to be trained to grow up; the urge to do so is innate. If he fails to pass out of childish or adolescent attitudes, this is because something has occurred to prevent the growth. Of course, he needs guidance and all the help that can be given him, but it must be directed to assisting him to become more fully himself.

The greatly increased flow of energy comes almost entirely from the sex instincts. It is for this reason that an understanding of infantile sexuality is important. The reproductive instincts, which impel the adult to courtship, mating, and the rearing of children, are extremely powerful, and directly or indirectly furnish the motives for a great part of every life. They seem able to override almost every other interest of men and women. They are the central theme of life. Even the unmarried tend to find their minds occupied with them, and if they are too heavily suppressed into the unconscious mind the consequences are usually disastrous for the mental health or the character of that individual. Just because they are so powerful and extensive in the adult, we are apt to think that the reproductive instincts with their immediate derivatives are the sole form of sex and that any apparent manifestations of sex in infancy were precocious and superficial and are now absorbed in the adult instincts.

This is a serious error. The sex or reproductive instincts of the adult are only one branch of the total of sexual instincts, admittedly a very important branch. In them the infantile sexual instincts have become merged to take a very specific form, prompting to the reproduction of the species. There is also a more general line of development from the infantile sex instincts, giving rise to impulses and interests that are not commonly recognized as sexual, because they do not seek satisfactions ordinarily associated with the meaning of that term.

We get into difficulties here over the use of the term, for if we reserve it to denote matters manifestly connected with the impulses and sentiments of the reproductive instincts, we seem to deny the connexion of these other nonspecific interests with sex; interests such as art, music, poetry, religion. It seems absurd at first sight to call these sexual, except when directly sexual matters enter into them, but the mental energy that motivates them comes from the same source as the energy of the sexual instincts that are clearly recognized as such. On the other hand, if we make the term 'sexual' too inclusive, it seems to lose sufficiently definite meaning and becomes a burdensome word making for confusion of thought and discussion.

I have referred to the specific adult sexual instincts as the reproductive instincts, because I did not wish to give the impression of excluding other possible sexual activities. What is more important than the use of terms (that, of course, cannot be regarded as unimportant) is that we should recognize the connexion existing between the specific sexual urges and sentiments and those other activities that have no specific 'sexual' aim, but nevertheless share a common source of energy with the sexual. If we look at them only in the adult, the connexion is by no means obvious. It is only when we trace the adult instincts back to their source in the period of infancy that we discover that these infantile roots also produced a secondary growth, differing in form from the specifically sexual.

The psychological mechanisms by which this growth is achieved are very complex. It is not necessary to trace them out here; an account of them can be had in any good book on the psychology of children. It is enough for our purposes to say that the process involves the desexualization of aim of the component sexual instincts, and that this sets the energy free to be used in other directions.

These need to have some connexion, by analogy, symbol, or association, with the primitive aim or object attachment of the instincts. For instance, an infantile sexual attachment to the mother or father can be detached, desexualized, and redirected to a parent substitute. The displacement can go through several stages, or be made to a number of different substitutes, and the end of the chain may be quite remote from the original attachment. It is rather like that word game sometimes played by children, in which by changing one letter at a time to give a new word the last word may be the reverse of the first, while each word resembles the one before it, for example, *Love, Dove, Dote, Date, Hate*. From mother to Church, or from father to God – by means of images and symbols, of course – is not such a reversal of meaning as this, and it is a transition easy to make for most people.

The development of the adolescent in religion must be seen in the light of this connexion between the reproductive sexual instincts and the non-specific derivative channels of desexualized energy. When the ripening of the reproductive instincts brings it great increase of energy, this flows through all the channels that have been formed, and the result is that there is a sharp quickening of interest in all the areas of feeling, not merely in the directly sexual.

Now that we have established clearly that they have a common origin in the sexuality of the infant, let us, for the sake of simplicity and clarity, call these secondary or derivative activities 'cultural', and use the term 'sexual' in the narrower adult sense of the word. A well-balanced personality must achieve maturity in these areas of life as well as in the sexual. Just as he has to grow from infantile and childhood sexuality to adult fullness, so must he grow out of the childhood attitudes in social and cultural life before he can take his proper place in society. He must grow up in religion, with which we are here specially concerned, and adolescence is a period of rapid growth.

The new energy, rising from the depths of the personality, on its way to new aims flows through the old channels and revives the infantile attachments. The family relationships, out of which he had passed from infancy to childhood, become emotionally significant again, and the objective preoccupation with the world, which characterized the intervening period of childhood, gives way to the exploration of his new emotions and a fresh interest in the parents as persons.

The Oedipus complex attitudes are faintly revived, but the barriers built at the end of infancy are adequate, in the normal development, to prevent the conflict reaching any great intensity. Instead, the phase passes quickly and the energy is led out from the family to find new ways of expressing itself. One of these ways leads to the discovery of new love objects, normally ending in marriage and the setting up of a home and family. The other ways lead to the cultural developments.

In this area, adolescence is marked by romanticism and idealism. This is compounded of the undefined memory of perfections carried over from infancy and of the sense of new worlds of experience lying ahead, ready to be explored. The infantile perfections are bound up in the parent images – the perfect satisfactions given by the mother, her unqualified beauty and devotion, and the greatness and power of the father, the absolute hero – but the intervening years of childhood have detached these images from the parents themselves, in the realism of childhood, and they remain in the background of the mind as images and complexes of feeling seeking an embodiment in the new world about to be discovered and conquered by the adolescent.

The urge to grow up into individual independence of personal being drives him to look for the perfections beyond the family at the same time as the new energy reactivates the ideals. In part the search governs his love life, especially in middle and later adolescence, and the beloved objects are seen through the screen of the infantile parent images and elicit the emotional fervour that the infant gave to his or her beloved parent, and they are not loved for themselves or seen as they are. But this is not enough. The search for perfection has to be carried into other fields.

We are concerned only with religion, but it must be remembered that this forms part of the general development of the adolescent and cannot be entirely separated from it or understood apart from it. Neglect of this principle has frequently led to pressures being put on adolescents to secure a degree of committal to religious attitudes that is premature for them. The emotional immaturity and instability that make it possible to achieve it fairly easily are the very reason why it is premature.

No Church is immune from this tendency in one way or another, but some sections of some Churches seem to regard it as a cardinal principle of religious education to press their young adherents to 'make a decision for the faith'. The effect of such pressure varies with every individual, but it runs two grave risks of jeopardizing full religious development – the risk of forced growth, and the risk of arrested growth.

The risk of forced growth comes from the rapid expansion of the emotions and imagination of the young adolescent. It is as though he were supplied by nature with riches that he must learn how to use to the best advantage. The mind is extremely complex, and in its growing stages does not develop evenly in all aspects. The balance comes only, when it comes, at maturity. In adolescence the intelligence and the accumulated experience of the world on which the intelligence depends are far outstripped by the emotional richness. Under the stimulus of the new forces at work inside him, the adolescent is beginning to seek new relationships with the world and a new understanding of it and of his place in it.

As we have seen, because he must start from where he is, mentally speaking, his search is to find the perfections and absolutes he unconsciously carries over from infancy. He must be given time to outgrow this phase if he is to attain to the deeper understanding of the meaning of life, and especially the religious life, which can only come when his emotions and his knowledge are better balanced. Religion offers perfections and absolutes, and if they are thrust strongly upon him, he will readily grasp at them and commit himself to them. This happens the more easily because another aspect of the renewal of infancy that comes in adolescence is hero-worship, and the influence of an admired religious teacher can sway him to make the decision. Moreover, the apparent absoluteness of his committal appeals strongly to his romanticism. In making it he gets the feeling of having found the meaning of life, the implicit aim of all striving after what is good and satisfying, and he wants to pour all his energies into this short-cut to perfection.

This is forced growth, because before many years the adolescent will find that he has oversimplified things. It is not so easy as it had seemed to recognize what is good among the complex and frequently conflicting demands made upon him by his environment and arising out of his effort to live in a world that is so very largely filled with activities and relationships that have little or no direct relationship with religion, the world of work and play and ordinary social intercourse. And he will have to fill his mind with learning that ignores or even seems to deny his religious preconceptions. His early self-committal to religion is challenged. In many people it stands up to the strain, for adolescents learn to adjust their religious ideas to include within them the new knowledge of the world and the new demands it makes upon them. With many others, however, the strain is too great. They can preserve their religious faith only by isolating it from the world; that is, by living in a narrow realm of ideas and emotions and denying by their behaviour that the world has any claim on them, or that it is in any way relevant to the truth of religious ideas. If they do not take this course of shutting their religion in a watertight compartment, they are likely to throw it overboard as a youthful illusion and become atheist or agnostic in their revolt from a religion that promised so great satisfactions and illumination, but failed to stand up to the test of a widening experience.

The second risk referred to just now lies in the moral field. When we were considering the development of the child in infancy, we saw that he emerges from infancy by forming a superego, which acts as a moral organ within the mind, passing judgement on the various impulses and ideas that spring up within the mind. The result of its action as critic and censor is to produce a sense of guilt over those impulses that it rejects. This is irrespective of whether they were carried into action or not, because at that stage the mind had not achieved a clear distinction between wish and reality. Adolescence brings a revival of infantile attitudes as the first stage of growing beyond them, and this comprises a revival of the severity of the superego. The young adolescent is more susceptible to guilt feelings than he was in the intermediate childhood period, and this guilt is likely to be associated with the new feelings of sex now developing within him. If he is subjected to strong teaching about sin and judgement, the action of his superego will be reinforced, and any decision he makes about committing himself to religion is likely to be of the negative, forbidding type discussed in an earlier chapter. His religion will be a protection to him against his natural impulses, not a means of transforming them into something positive. His development will be arrested, for his superego will then not allow him to grow beyond this stage, for every effort to do so will call up a sense of guilt, both conscious and unconscious.

It will be remembered that in discussing the formation of the superego, it was pointed out that girls emerge from infancy with a less strongly developed superego than that which normally is formed in boys. Because of this, the risk to which we have been drawing attention is less for them than for boys. The risk of forced growth is present with them, but as the two risks usually operate together, high-pressure religion is on the whole less likely to do hurt to them than it is to boys. This does not mean that it is desirable, for it always involves some distortion of growth.

The kind of teaching here referred to is that which aims at some form of conversion of an emotional or dramatic kind in adolescents. Another form of teaching likely to produce analogous bad effects is that which lays great emphasis on sin, guilt, punishment, and expiation of guilt by suffering. This, too, will produce a superego religion in which God is basically pictured after the pattern of the bad father image, and its characteristic note will be that of duty towards God and one's neighbour, rather than of love. It will frequently have an element of masochism; that is, of delight in suffering, because suffering eases the burden of guilt this kind of religion tends to create in its followers. It sees virtue in 'a heart resigned, submissive, meek', rather than in the faith that 'I can do all things through Christ who strengtheneth me'.

These are some of the dangers confronting the adolescent who is subjected to religious training in the hands of those who implicitly or explicitly take the attitude that religion is something that has to be imposed or grafted upon the growing personality. At every stage of the child's development this attitude is likely to do him harm, so far as religion is concerned. But it does not follow that there should not be religious teaching offered to the adolescent boy or girl. He greatly needs it, but needs it not as a protection against the welter of new impulses springing up inside himself, but to help him to develop them into full flowering in a united and balanced personality. Such teaching will make use of the two chief marks of adolescence, the new emotional development and the urge to independence.

The first of these shows itself in idealism in the abstract, and hero-worship in the concrete, the idealism resulting from the effort to rediscover in the world the lost perfections of infancy, and the hero-worship from the revivification of the parent images and the search for people to fit them. Because the religion of the adolescent must build upon these, any religious teaching that is given needs to be of such a nature as to draw them out.

It must also take account of the second mark of adolescence, which is in some ways the opposite of the first. The urge to independence shows itself as a search for self-expression, or self-discovery, on the part of the adolescent. He wants to go his own way, and becomes impatient of restrictions placed upon him. He is dissatisfied with second-hand ideas, critical of the teaching of his elders, convinced that they are out of date and old-fashioned. To their eyes he is frequently rebellious and wild, accepting lowered moral standards if not even openly immoral. That is a common charge raised against the younger generation at every epoch. So we are apt to get two contrasting pictures of adolescents, one depicting them as dreamy-eyed, moody, gangling, easily led away by unrealistic enthusiasms, and the other making them appear as lawless, rebellious, uncontrollable, almost (if not quite) delinquents.

Both views of the adolescent are apt to be exaggerated by adults, particularly when they are not balanced against each other as they ought to be. Most adolescents reveal both, sometimes alternately, sometimes simultaneously, as they are to be expected in normal growth. Maturity will bring an integration of the two, harnessing the drive of rebelliousness into a positive pursuit of the new ideals that have been brought into closer relationship to the actualities of the world and that contain less fantasy.

The aim of religious training at this stage should be to foster this growth towards maturity and the integration of the two trends. Unfortunately, religious teachers are frequently liable to be impatient with the young; to condemn their rebelliousness and to criticize their dreaminess – though sometimes they try to lead the latter into the wrong channels of a religiosity that splits off the spiritual visionary drive from the urge to action, and in this way hinders the integration. But by recognizing that the two trends really belong together as valuable stages of growth, religious training can help greatly in the forward movement. Indeed, religion may be the only thing that can bring about the complete integration.

In the first place, religion will be presented as an adventure. It is a challenge to devote one's life to the service of God and of good. Good causes abound in the battle against the giant enemies of civilization and the welfare of man – ignorance, disease, poverty, squalor, greed, and all the rest. To attack these is to find a real purpose in life; it should not be presented just as a duty to be accepted. The positive aspects of the Kingdom of God need to be put in the forefront as an ideal to inspire to real achievement. The new energies springing up in the adolescent are creative in nature, and they can be drawn into channels of creative action. The adventure is not merely one of action; it is also an adventure of the mind and spirit. New worlds of thought open up to be explored, new ways of living to be discovered, and always, just beyond the threshold, seems to lie the secret of life. The young are always seeking goodness, even in their badness or delinquency. The search after God is the greatest of all adventures, but it is only gradually that the adolescent comes to the full realization of what this means.

The presentation of this challenge has to be made at first in concrete terms, that is, by the example of social, moral, spiritual, and religious heroes of the past and present. In today's world, the example of Albert Schweitzer is worth an infinity of sermons and classes in helping the young to understand the inner spirit of religion as adventure. The concrete example of the great heroes of mankind serves not only to make it easier to grasp the meaning of the ideal; it also provides the bridge by which the young attain to it. We grow by identification, as was pointed out earlier in this book, and to have the actual example before him makes it easier for the adolescent to live for the time being in the person of the hero, to fill his mind with pictures of himself doing the same thing, and to make such ideals a dynamic part of his own self. He becomes in part the hero whom he worships for the time being, and this remains as a permanent influence in shaping his final development. The teaching of Scripture should be presented in the same way, as an exposition of life rather than of doctrine. In Jeremiah or Isaiah, in Peter and Paul, and above all in Jesus, is to be seen what it means to have a great vision of God and his Kingdom, and to strive after it. And in the presentation of love as the great religious impulse, we speak direct to the innate meaning of the adolescent's new urges. All this opens the way to the recognition of religion as the fullest understanding of the world, and shows it as the way by which we rise to the fullness of life and the attainment of true power.

This idealism that aspires to the realization of a new world, [illegible] heaven, needs a corrective; it needs to be anchored in the world. The second trend of adolescence must find full scope. This is the growth to independence and freedom, freedom even from primary bondage to God. The adolescent will go astray unless he develops a sound ability to criticize. He begins by his criticism of his elders and his revolt from their authority over him and from acceptance of their opinions and their values. Far from being discouraged from doing this, he needs to be encouraged to find his own values and test the truth of all beliefs. If he is hindered or opposed in his criticism of others, he will seldom advance far enough to be critical of himself. He will at best only become distrustful of himself, and grow cynical or indifferent.

Religious ideas can be taught, but the truth of religion can only be discovered; and it is far more important to foster the spirit of discovery – which is the response to the challenge to adventure – than to persuade adolescents to accept without question what their teachers tell them. We should in many cases go so far as to encourage an active distrust, at least a questioning, of the accepted religious beliefs. Only so will these become strong enough, and enough part of the person, to be able to stand the tests to which they will be subjected by everyday life in the world; and only so will they become a taking-off point for further progress into the realm of the spirit.

So, with the attainment of spiritual freedom, made possible by the support and encouragement of a society of free persons who trust him, the adolescent comes to his maturity and is ready to take his full part in that same society and in turn to help the free growth of the younger persons who come under his care, as their parent, their teacher, their pastor, or simply as their friend. His religious development, though far from ended, has come to its maturity of form.

INDEX